Acknowledgments

WHAT WE BECOME IN GOD is a sum total of the divine encounters we have had, the people we have met, our experiences, and the books we have read. The saying "No man is an island" is certainly true in the context of authoring this book. I want to acknowledge the impact that the following men and women of God have had on my life: Dr. Jonathan David (my father in the faith), Apostle Harrison Chileshe (my pastor), Apostle John Eckhardt (who introduced me to the apostolic), Dr. John P. Kelly (who commissioned me as an apostle), Dr. Nick Castellano (for his insights in BioChemistry), Robert Ricciardelli, Prophet Kevin Leal (my big brother), Pastor Frank Rosenstein (my business partner), Dr. G.E. Bradshaw (my covenant brother), Danny Seay (who has become a living example of this book's message) Larry Favalora (for being a true Joseph), Bishop Robert Smith (who introduced me to the message on the One New Man), Dr Jay Simms, Dr. Paula Price, Apostles Pam Vinnett and Cheryl Fortson—their teachings and personal conversations with me over the years have added to the richness of this book.

While the material in this book is original, there are a few quotes throughout that have been taken from the published works of other notable Christian authors, which add depth to the topic or focus. Each is documented in the Endnote section.

Hall of Appreciation

"The Lord gave the word: great was the company of those that published it."
Psalm 68:11 KJV

IT HAS BEEN SAID that great projects are never the work of one man, but the collective effort of a team that shares a common destiny. I want to give a heartfelt "God bless you" to the following brothers and sisters for making the publishing of this book a reality. May God give you a tremendous harvest for every person who will be transformed by the truths contained within.

Trina Myles (my best friend, wife and partner in the business of the Kingdom)

Teri Secrest (my student and business partner). Thank you Teri for believing in me and the message that I bring to the Body of Christ. Thanks a million times for funding the first printing of this book.

Endorsements

Finally someone has taken the challenge of answering the voices that has echoed throughout time, asking why me, and how can I stop what I have always seen and "promised to never become" and it happened anyway. The voice of agony has finally found rest and comfort through this riveting book written by Dr. Frances Myles, *Breaking Generational Curses under the Order of Melchizedek*. This book calm nerves as it educates us to the mastery of generational victories. This daring piece of artwork reveals the heart of Jesus and brings conclusions to hopeless cries and desperations in the midnight hour of our lives. Finally the dawn of a new day has arrived, as curses are destroyed permanently and future generations can rise with dimensional victories, and each generation progressing in these victories. This book stimulates the pulse of God in grasping real lineage and taking it to the next level. A definite must have in your library because you will never, ever be the same after reading this book.

— Apostle Helen Saddler
Presiding Prelate and Founder
Into His Chambers Ministries, Int'l
Kent, Washington

"Though I have both benefitted personally and participated in deliverance ministry, at some level there always seemed to be more under the surface. Some sort of access that often allowed those I had seen set free to easily become entangled again. I had never given much thought to the legality of the action, and the rights given generationally through sin to access us today. By legally receiving our rights to be free through being joined with Christ as His bride, this access is once and for all broken! My experience post participating in this process through Dr. Myles seminar has been an experience of freedom beyond words. My life has taken on a new sense of joy that can only be explained by the lack of access the enemy has through my familial line, and my heart being joined at an even deeper to Christ. Dr. Myles has found a spiritual key that will unlock the chains of many for the

Fathers Kingdom purpose in their lives. I highly recommend everyone experience this personally. You will not be left the same."

> – Jeffrey Szakonyi
> *Pastor/Speaker/ Businessman*
> *Co-Owner/Director of Sales and Marketing*
> *Cameo Strings, LLC*
> *www.rockonfashions.com*
> *jeffrey@cameostrings.com*

Table of Contents

Preface xi

Chapter One
Ancient Pathways 1

Chapter Two
Roots and Origins 13

Chapter Three
Man's Original Prophetic DNA 25

Chapter Four
Demonic Genetic Mutation 35

Chapter Five
Understanding Generational Curses 49

Chapter Six
The Anatomy of a Generational Curse 57

Chapter Seven
The Law of Inheritance 65

Chapter Eight
Supernatural Genetic Reconfiguration 73

Chapter Nine
The Order of Melchizedek 81

Chapter Ten
How to Retire Generational Curses Permanently 93

Chapter Eleven
The Generational Blessing 105

Chapter Twelve
Testimonial Case Studies 113

Chapter Thirteen
The 12 Ancient Oils of Scripture 119

Foreword

Once again Dr. Francis Myles captures the very essence of the Power, Dominion and Authority we as followers of Christ have on this planet and how that Power when wielded properly can break generational curses in our life and the life of our family. Utilizing, Biochemistry, Quantum Physics and the Word, Dr. Myles has given the reader the "how to" tools to teach them how to step into that power and break those generational curses or "mindsets" passed down thru the DNA. Dr. Myles shares with the reader a "failsafe" spiritual technology that is reproducible and works time and time again when wielded properly in the unseen spiritual realm to overturn and restore the human genome to it's original pure self created by our father God "in the beginning". By teaching these tools and explaining them in detail in both scientific and spiritual terms Dr Myles helps free the reader of any mental bondage by having the reader step back into his "son-ship" thru the Order of Melchizedek restored to us by Jesus Christ.

I highly recommend this book to both the intellectual and spiritually minded to be guided on how to utilize this power that God has restored to us on this planet through Jesus Christ..

Yours In Christ,
Dr. Nick Castellano
(Bio-Chemist/Nuclear Chemist)

I will praise thee, for I am fearfully and wonderfully made: Marvellous are thy works; and that my soul knoweth right well.

Psalm 139:14

Mankind is God's most marvelous creation, and in fact, the only one made in His image and in His likeness. Because of this fact, we are unique beings and have special importance in the scheme of creation. We are designed to rule and govern planet Earth as God' powerful ambassadors. However, we have an enemy to that process...sin. Because of sin, mankind lost his territorial authority over this planet. Sin entered the human bloodline and began to spread like a plague throughout the biological network of human existence. All appeared to be lost and the question would be... "Can mankind ever regain his noble authority on this planet and can he once again have the eternal relationship that he needs with his creator God?"

The answer to these questions is "yes," and through the restorative power of Jesus Christ we have done just that. Most believers understand the redemptive power of Christ, but most don't know how great the benefits of the restorative power of Christ's blood are. This power reaches to levels that before now may have been untapped for many. The origins of any thing, living or inanimate tell a powerful story of how to govern or use such a thing to its fullest extent. There are discoveries to be made. Being able to trace our supernatural origins to our restored place in Christ reveals powerful information that will alter our lives forever. This power affects us on spiritual "sub-atomic levels."

In the 1980's there was a television series called "The Six Million Dollar Man." A man was injured in an accident and was clinging to life. The doctors and scientists collaborated on the process of his restoration. They said "We can rebuild him...better, stronger, faster...than he was before." In a sense, we are in fact, "genetically altered" beings...God's "Six-million Dollar Men and Women" so to speak. God has rebuilt us in Christ...better, faster, stronger!

My covenant brother, Dr. Francis Myles has uncovered and explained one of the greatest mysteries of the "New Man" that has ever been revealed. In this powerful book he reveals the supernatural "genetic restoration" of born-again mankind, showing us levels of victory that seemed impossible before. You will not be able to keep from being intrigued and intensely motivated to move to new levels of personal and corporate victory. You will find yourself tackling the issues that you steered clear of before, believing that they were things you just had to "live with."

Now, victory has come in a new way in this Biblically accurate and powerful book, *"Breaking Generational Curses under the Order of Melchizedek!"*

– Dr. Gordon E. Bradshaw
Governing Apostle
Global Effect Ministries Network
Director - The "ACTivity Institute" - Center for
Kingdom Empowerment

PREFACE

From antiquity to the present time men and women from all walks of life have inherently understood that the past does affect the present and future order of things. This inherent knowledge may explain why the expression "Like father, like son" is both common and universal. I once overheard women gossiping about the village drunk... "young Johnny has also become a hopeless drunkard just like his father and grandfather were. Every member of this young man's family has been a hopeless alcoholic for as long as I could remember."

Unfortunately this casual social acknowledgement of the reality of repetitive behavior; whether it is good or bad in humans who are related by bloodline trivializes, one of the most scientific and spiritually complex phenomenon in human history. The recent amazing advancements in Biochemistry, Quantum Physics and Genetic science have given us a front row seat in the world of DNA. Scientists are deeply awed by the amazing divine complexities of the human genome.

Scientists and Biochemists are baffled by the amount of information about a person's character, ability and inherent destiny that can be contained in a single strand of DNA. There is great consensus within the scientific community that the human genome is a rich instructional reservoir concerning all that is needed to be known about the person whose DNA is under investigation. What is certain is that any kind of security breach to the integrity of any strand of DNA within the human genome can affect any individual negatively.

By understanding the dynamics of DNA within the human genome Scientists can explain to some degree many things. For example: Why does a fourth generation grandson of a dead great grandfather, who was an alcoholic when he was alive, also struggle with the same addictions to alcohol as his progenitor. But, when it comes to the study of "Genetic engineering and mutation" Biochemists are limited to what they are able to understand by their carnal observations. The Bible is clear that all life forms have a spiritual template behind their visible dynamics.

Through faith we understand that the worlds were framed by the word of God, so that things which are seen were not made of things which do appear.
                                                                    Hebrews 11:3 KJV

The above passage is clear that every visible element in creation is a byproduct of spiritual technology. This means that all visible elements in creation, including DNA (the human genome), are affected by the dimensions of the spirit world. This also means that the genetics of any person's bloodline can be affected by God's creative power or be infected by manipulation from demonic powers and death agencies. The Genetic mutation that is caused by demonic manipulation of the human genome is the underlying essence of this book.

This invisible but malignant manipulation of human DNA by evil spirits, with diabolical assignments, is what this book is going to address. The diabolical manipulation of the human genome by demonic powers over many generations is a spiritual phenomenon commonly known as "Generation Curses."

By definition, *Generational Curses* are curses or iniquities that are perpetuated in repeated behavior cycles over several generations. What is of note is that the phenomenon of *Generational Curses* does not track learned behavior, but traces patterns of behavior on a subconscious and genetic level. How else do you explain the circumstance of a woman who grows up under a very abusive father? She promises herself that she will never marry an abusive man like her father. But when she finally says, "I do" it is to a man exactly like her own father. How do you describe a young man who is constantly coming to the rescue of his mother against a physically abusive father? He promises himself that he will never physically abuse his future wife but he becomes physically abusive after saying "I do."

I wish could say that *Kingdom Citizens* (born again Disciples of Christ) are not subject to the above demonically engineered malignant phenomenon. I wish I could say that born again believers cannot be affected by the tyranny of *Generational Curses*. But, widespread experience has blown this theory out of the ballpark. To make this subject even more personal, I am the former victim of this insidious genetic phenomenon. I saw widespread genetic patterns of behavior in my own natural lineage (bloodline) that I loathed intensely but ended up doing myself. For some of these behaviors, the fact that I was a born again God-fearing child of God did little to stop these subconscious behaviors in me.

A couple of years ago, I saw the Texas Department of Justice haul off a dear brother in Christ to jail. He is serving a 45year prison sentence as a pedophile, because he molested two of his young nieces, in a moment of genetic indiscretion. By all accounts, this brother was a God-fearing man who loved his wife and children dearly. The man's wife asked me to give this dear brother in Christ a pastoral visit, while he was waiting sentencing. A tear drenched and repentant man told me how he hated himself for what he had done. It was clear that he was deeply ashamed of his abominable sexual violation of minors. Deeper investigation into his indiscretion revealed the following facts:

- There was a long history of child pedophilia in his bloodline

- There was also a long of history of lingering mental depression in his lineage

- The brother had been taking a powerful drug that helped to deeply suppress both his mental depression and his insidious sexual attraction to minors.

- The day that he sexually molested two of his nieces was the day that he had refused to take his medication. The medication that helped him also left him with other disturbing side effects.

I want to go on record as saying that I do not condone any form of child pedophilia or the sexual exploitation of minors. But through the gospel of Christ, I have a lot of compassion for believers and sinners alike who are losing their fight to deeply embedded genetic anomalies.

The billion-dollar question that this book will attempt to answer is simply this:

Is there a failsafe spiritual technology for destroying, overturning and reversing demonically engineered mutations in the human genome?

Answering this question is the underlying essence and objective for writing this book. After I wrote my book <u>The Order of Melchizedek</u>, and launched the order of Melchizedek Leadership University to train kingdom citizens and kingdom entrepreneurs, I discerned a very deep interest in the in the last module of the live classes. The last module in our school of Ministry is titled *"Breaking Generational Curses under the Order of Melchizedek."* Many of our students experienced dramatic breakthroughs, after I prayed for them in accordance with the truths contained in this book. Because of those breakthroughs, they began to beg me to write a book on the subject.

The book that you are now holding in your hands is a result of my desire to place this revelation into the hands of my students who have attended our Leadership University. It is also my humble attempt to reach out to God-fearing believers in the body of Christ who are tired of wrestling with demonically engineered genetic anomalies.

                Yours for kingdom advancement

– Dr. Francis Myles
Senior Pastor: *Breakthrough City Kingdom Embassy (www.breakthroughcity.com)*
Chancellor: *The Order of Melchizedek Leadership University ("http://www.theomlu.com")*
CEO: *Kingdom Marketplace Coalition LLC (www.mykmcportal.com)*

Chapter One

ANCIENT PATHWAYS

I once hosted a world renowned Brain Scientist at my church in Texas named Dr Aiko Hormann. She made a statement that stuck with me: "In the scientific community, any book that is older than two years is considered outdated because of the rapid advancements in both technology and science." This statement helped me to appreciate why many scientists struggle with the concept of basing their faith on a book (the Bible), which contains ancient scrolls on life, science and faith. I immediately began to contrast Dr Aiko Hormann's statement about the scientific community with the following scripture from the book of Jeremiah:

> *Because my people hath forgotten me, they have burned incense to vanity, and they have caused them to stumble in their **ways** from the **ancient** paths, to walk in paths, in a way not cast up;*
>
> Jeremiah 18:15

In Defense of the Ancient Pathways

In the above passage of scripture God gives us His own diagnosis for why His covenant people (Israel) were failing to walk in the favor of His presence. God accuses His covenant people of...

- Forgetting Him.

- Worshiping worthless idols.

- Walking in pathways that have never been proven in the context of His predetermined will for their lives.

God concludes His diagnosis of Israel's spiritual ills, by showing them the underlying root cause behind their failure to walk in the favor of His presence and His predetermined purpose for their life. God tells the children of Israel that they had forgotten about the ancient paths that God had established for their benefit, before the foundation of the world.

God's diagnosis and prognosis for ancient Israel's spiritual, social and economic ills still holds true for our High Tech and scientifically advanced modern societies. The primary reason this is so, is because all of creation was created on the tapestry of God's eternal wisdom. No amount of technological and scientific discovery can override or overshadow the incredible wisdom of God. This is why Dr Aiko Hormann's favorite expression is: "Science is catching up with the Bible."

Before the dawn of the fifteenth century, many scientific scholars believed that the earth was flat and that the Sun and Moon revolved around the earth. But in 1522 explorer Ferdinand Magellan finally provided first-hand proof that this idea was not correct, by being the first person to sail completely around the Earth. After Ferdinand Magellan's voyage, the theory of a flat earth dissipated into the thin air. Scientific consensus convened and settled around the fact that a circular earth orbits around our Sun.

While this scientific discovery was very exhilarating for the 14th century scientific community, their discovery was not breaking news within the ancient Hebrew text. A righteous Prophet and a God-fearing businessman by the names of Isaiah and Job (who lived thousands of years ago) had already discovered, by divine revelation that the earth was round, or circular. This righteous Prophet, and this God-fearing businessman, had beat Ferdinand Magellan (by 14 centuries) on his so-called historic discovery.

> *God sits above the circle of the earth. The people below seem like grasshoppers to him! He spreads out the heavens like a curtain and makes his tent from them.*
> Isaiah 40:22

> *He has placed an enclosing limit [the horizon] upon the waters at the boundary between light and darkness.*
> Job 26:10 AMP

Curiously, many astronomy textbooks credit Pythagoras (c. 570–500 B.C.) with being the first person to assert that the earth was round. However, the Biblical passages are older than this. Isaiah is generally acknowledged to have been written in the area of 700 B.C. Job is thought to have been written around

2000 B.C. The secular astronomers, before the time of Pythagoras, must have thought that the Bible was wrong about its teaching of a round earth. Yet, the Bible was exactly right. It was the secular science of the day that needed to be corrected. (Taking Back Astronomy by Dr. Jason Lisle)

Ancient Pathways and Universal Theory

We will explore some passages of Scripture which touch upon the topics of astronomy and astrophysics. It is interesting that many of the Bible's statements about astronomy went against the generally accepted teachings of the time. Undoubtedly, many of these verses would have seemed counterintuitive, and may have been difficult to believe when they were first written. However, modern science has confirmed what the Bible has taught. As in all things, the Bible is absolutely correct when it teaches about the universe. The Bible indicates that the earth is round. Consider Isaiah 40:22 which mentions the "circle of the earth." This description is certainly fitting. When the earth is viewed from space it always appears as a circle, since it is round. Another verse that indicates the spherical nature of our planet is Job 26:10. This verse teaches that God has inscribed a circle on the surface of the waters at the boundary of light and darkness. This boundary between light and darkness (day and night) is called the "terminator" since the light stops or "terminates" there. Someone standing on the terminator would be experiencing either a sunrise or a sunset. In other words, they are either going from day to night or from night to day. The terminator is always a circle, because the earth is round. (Taking Back Astronomy by Dr. Jason Lisle)

What is adamantly clear from the majority of recorded geological, biological and scientific discoveries is the complete and amazing consistency of the ancient pathways of the ancient Hebrew Scriptures. They give us an accurate diagnosis and prognosis for faith, science and life. In more cases than not, what we are celebrating as the most amazing scientific breakthroughs of our time, are simply the rediscovering of what God had already embedded into the eternal tapestry of creation many milleniums ago. I recently had a very refreshing talk with a very brilliant Quantum Physicist and Biochemist who is also a man of faith. He told me that the field of Quantum Physics is causing many scientists to reevaluate their long held beliefs against matters of faith. Quantum Physicists are rediscovering the unmistakable signature of a super intelligent designer in the tapestry of creation. As advancements in Quantum

Physics reaches its zenith it will soon become a taboo for Quantum Physicists to not believe in the existence of God.

God stretches the northern sky over empty space and hangs the earth on nothing.
Job 26:7

In the above passage, Job, the successful first century holy businessman who was a true friend of God, had also discovered (via divine revelation), that the earth orbits in the voidness of space hanging onto nothing.

A very interesting verse to consider is Job 26:7, it states that God "hangs the earth on nothing." This might evoke an image of God hanging the earth as if it were a Christmas tree ornament. But, He hung the earth on empty space. This verse expresses in a poetic way the fact that the earth is unsupported by any other object, something quite unnatural for the ancient writers to imagine. Indeed, the earth does float in space. We now have pictures of the earth, taken from space, that show it floating in the cosmic void. The earth literally hangs on nothing, just as the Bible teaches. (Taking Back Astronomy by Dr. Jason Lisle)

Divine Predestination

For we are God's [own] handiwork (His workmanship), recreated in Christ Jesus, [born anew]that we may do those good works which God predestined (planned beforehand) for us [taking paths which He prepared ahead of time], that we should walk in them [living the good life which He prearranged and made ready for us to live].
Ephesians 2:10 AMP

One subject that causes much debate among theologians is the subject of Divine Predestination. But, the subject of Divine Predestination should never be a subject that arouses contentious debates. Divine Predestination in its very essence is pretty simple. As a matter of definition, the word predestination is made up of two English words: "Pre" which means "before" and "Destination." Divine Predestination therefore simply means: "To set the destination beforehand."

The apostle Paul in Ephesians 2:10 tells us that we are God's workmanship, created in Christ Jesus, unto good works, that God had predestinated for us to walk in. Since God never starts anything until He is finished, we have to ask ourselves a very important question:

How did God preprogram us to walk in the ancient paths that he had prepared for us from before the foundation of the world?

The deep and far-reaching technological and scientific advancements in biochemistry have unmasked how God, in His eternal genius, preprogrammed mankind to fulfill His predetermined purposes. God deposited His instructions concerning the fulfillment of His eternal purposes in our DNA.

Before Adam and Eve committed high treason against God in the garden, they had the best DNA of any human being who has ever lived on earth, apart from Christ. Adam and Eve's original DNA, before the sin nature crept into our human nature, was an amazing reservoir of Divine revelation concerning the future destiny. Understanding this fact alone, will help us to unveil the mystery of Ephesians 2:10.

Ancient Pathways in the Human Genome

What becomes increasingly clear from examining Ephesians 2:10 (and other similar passages from the Bible), is that God in His genius planted the ancient pathways inside the human genome or DNA. Before they fell from glory, the first kingdom ambassadors did not need the services of a prophet to tell them what they needed to do for God. This is because the mystery of God's perfect will for their life, and destiny, was deeply encoded in their DNA. Their DNA was like the microchip of a supercomputer with deeply embedded divine instructions, and spiritual pathways that would have enabled them to become the true manifest sons of God, here on earth. How God created Adam and Eve's original DNA is nothing short of genius. Only an intelligent God is able to wire such deeply embedded genetic instructions into His creation.

> *Because my people hath forgotten me, they have burned incense to vanity, and they have caused them to stumble in their **ways** from the **ancient** paths, to walk in paths, in a way not cast up;*
>
> Jeremiah 18:15

When we re-examine the passage in Jeremiah 18:15, from the genetic standpoint, this creature takes on a whole new meaning. We begin to see that God is speaking about the ancient pathways from many levels. When the apostle John was on the island of Patmos he had a powerful vision of the resurrected Christ. John tells us that the voice of Christ was like the sound of many waters.

Having been born in a country that is famous for the Victoria Falls, I know what the sound of many waters sounds like. It is like sound waves vibrating at different frequencies. John's description of Christ voice implies that God speaks on many levels. Armed with this understanding, what is the true essence of Jeremiah 18:15?

Let us suppose that God is speaking to the people of Israel first and foremost, at a genetic level. The ancient paths, in this case, would have to be God's original genetic pathways that He had established, in the DNA of His covenant people. Forensic scientists and biochemists will be the first ones to tell you that the human genome is made up of millions of wires, or connective tissues, called DNA strands. Each of these strands of DNA, according to scientists, can contain vast amounts of encoded instructions. They are designed to mitigate the behavior of the person whose DNA is under investigation. Since these DNA strands are already encoded with deeply embedded genetic instruction (that governs how a person behaves, desires and functions; that were never put the in the DNA by the scientists), we would have to conclude that many of these genetic instructions are divinely embedded. The supernatural restoration and reconfiguration of these long-lost ancient pathways, of God in man's genetic makeup, is what this book is all about.

Let us now suppose that Jeremiah 18:15, in its second embassy, deals with the restoration of the ancient pathways of the Spirit in our spiritual walk. In this second embassy, this passage of Scripture would then have us focus on the restoration of kingdom principles and concepts that would enable us to represent God fully here on earth. Besides the demonic breach in our human genome (that forces us to fight with deeply embedded genetic tendencies), we will also discuss in this book spiritual principles that will help us to break free of the phenomenon known as generational curses.

Breaking through Demonic Barricades

And when he was come to the other side into the country of the Gergesenes, there met him two possessed with devils, coming out of the tombs, exceeding fierce, so that no man might pass by that way.

Matthew 8:28

One of the things that I am trusting God to do, for those who are reading this book, is to help you break through demonically engineered barriers (whether they be spiritual, mental or genetic). The prophetic picture of what I see concerning breaking through demonic barriers on a mental and genetic level is found in Matthew 8:28. This passage of Scripture has always fascinated me. Jesus Christ took his disciples across the sea into the country of the Gergesenes. When Christ got on shore He took a pathway that was protected by two very violent demoniacs. The devil had positioned two very violent and intimidating evil spirits in these two demoniacs. No human being ever dared to take this pathway. But Christ was not intimidated by the demonic display of violence. To the contrary, Christ came to this region with the specific intent of challenging these two demonic powers for the rights to this valuable pathway.

Think about this: The devil, unlike God, is not omnipresent. This means that the devil, and his confederacy of spirits, cannot be everywhere at the same time. Like any Army general with limited resources, the devil has to be very strategic about where he places his resources and where he does not place them. Why would the devil invest in stationing two very violent spirits to protect a pathway that was of little or no value? I truly believe that this pathway, in the country of the Gergesenes, must have been of high spiritual value to both the kingdom of God and the kingdom of darkness. Christ Jesus, in His holy majesty, would never have bothered to fight for a pathway that was of no spiritual significance.

Consequently, what is the prophetic significance of this passage from Matthew 8:28? I believe that the prophetic significance of this passage is that it shows us that there are strategic spiritual pathways, of the Spirit, that God embedded into our human genome. These ancient pathways that the devil guards jealously and violently can lead us to great spiritual and natural breakthroughs, if we recapture them. I really believe that one of those ancient pathways, that the devil guards jealously, is the spiritual pathway of God that contains our destiny code. This code is embedded in our genetics. The devil does not want us to rediscover the prophetic wiring of God's purposes and plans for our life. God stored those plans in the original prophetic DNA (Sonship DNA) that He planted in Adam, our human progenitor. But, I am trusting God, that the prophetic revelation contained in this book is going to help you break through the veil of demonic violence. You too can recapture God's original prophetic DNA for your life.

The Immutability of the Ancient Pathways

I know that, whatsoever God doeth, it shall be for ever: nothing can be put to it, nor any thing taken from it: and God doeth it, that men should fear before him. That which hath been is now; and that which is to be hath already been; and God requireth that which is past.

Ecclesiastes 3:14-15

Ecclesiastes 3:14-15 is a very interesting passage of Scripture that I want us to dissect, in the context of the subject of this book. This passage of Scripture from King Solomon, the wisest and richest man who has ever lived, cements the importance and immutability of the ancient pathways of God. King Solomon tells us that the ancient pathways of God are immutable and eternal, whether they exist as immutable laws in the tapestry of creation, or as prophetically wired divine instructions in the human genome.

Listed below in bullet points is the nomenclature of the ancient pathways of God, based upon Ecclesiastes 3:14-15.

- All the ancient pathways of God begin with God and are powered by God.

- All the ancient pathways of God are eternal and unchangeable.

- All the ancient pathways of God are the foundational and governing principles of God, that are embedded in the tapestry of creation.

- All the ancient pathways of God were designed to bridge the gap between heaven and earth; and to bridge the gap between eternity, time and space.

The immutability and unchangeableness, of the ancient pathways of God, form the foundation for any form of credible science. It would be practically impossible for scientists to attach any credible scientific device to unpredictable laws of nature.

Sin and the devil, who is a prisoner of Sin, are no match for a man or woman who rediscovers the ancient pathways of God, and builds their life around these ancient paths. This is why the discovery of the ancient pathways of God in nature, and in our genetics, is the devil's worst nightmare.

The Prophetic Implications of God's Foreknowledge

The Lord gave me this message: "I knew you before I formed you in your mother's womb. Before you were born I set you apart an first and appointed you as my prophet to the nations."

Jeremiah 1:4-5

Before concluding this chapter on the ancient pathways of God, I want us to examine the prophetic implications of God's foreknowledge, on the subject of this book. In the previous paragraph we examined the immutability of the ancient pathways of God. What we did not examine is the spiritual element that causes the ancient pathways of God to be immutable. This spiritual element, which is behind the immutability of the ancient pathways of God, is a factor known as God's foreknowledge. This factor is also known as the God factor because it is only found in God.

For I know the plans I have for you," says the Lord. "They are plans for good and not for disaster, to give you a future and a hope.

Jeremiah 29:11

Jeremiah 1:5 and Jeremiah 29:11 give us a prophetic synopsis of this supernatural element called God's foreknowledge.

God's foreknowledge is His inherent ability to know all things, at any given moment. It is His divine ability to know the end from the beginning. There are no experiments in anything that God ever does, God's foreknowledge affords Him the eternal luxury of 100% precision in everything that He does, or creates. The prophetic implications of God's foreknowledge are that *God never does anything outside the eternal counsel of His foreknowledge.*

The prophetic or spiritual implications of the above statements are truly deep and far-reaching. Since God never does anything outside the eternal counsel of His foreknowledge, it means that when God first created the human genome (DNA); the divine instructions (about our personality profile, potential, assignments and destiny that God had inserted inside our DNA strands), were all based upon His foreknowledge. Outside of external demonically engineered interference, our genetic makeup was divinely primed to cause us to walk out our God given destiny. This means that they were able to walk out their destiny without the aid of external stimuli such as prophecy or preaching. But this is not the experience of most born-again followers of Christ around the world. Many believers seem to be in constant need of external stimulus (such as prophecy, teaching or preaching), in order to walk out their God given destiny.

> *Indeed, the Sovereign Lord never does anything until he reveals his plans to his servants the prophets.*
>
> Amos 3:7

I believe in prophets and prophecy because the testimony of Jesus Christ is the spirit of prophecy. But when I was writing this book the Holy Spirit told me that "Son, Amos 3:7 only became necessary after the fall of Adam and Eve. Had Adam and Eve not sinned in the Garden, and compromised their God given prophetic DNA, there would have been no need for prophets on earth!" I was both stunned and moved by what the Holy Spirit told me. Man's original DNA (Genetic code) was like a preprogrammed nuclear missile with specific inbuilt operational protocols and target coordinates. Said in another way, man's original prophetic (Sonship) DNA contained every prophecy about his person and future.

Breaking Generational Curses under the Order of Melchizedek is a prophetic book about the supernatural restoration of man's original prophetic (Sonship) DNA through the finished work of Christ. This book will examine an ancient eternal spiritual order called The *Order of Melchizedek*, which is headed by the Lord Jesus Christ. This ancient order holds answers for today's mind-boggling challenges. Unlike scientists, who believe that the answers to the world's problems are predicated on future scientific breakthroughs, God's Kingdom operates on the premise that all the answers to today's problems (and the future), are found in rediscovering His ancient paths. God wired those paths into the fabric of creation eons of years ago.

ANCIENT PATHWAYS

LIFE APPLICATION SECTION

MEMORY VERSE

For we are God's [own] handiwork (His workmanship), recreated in Christ Jesus, [born anew] that we may do those good works which God predestined (planned beforehand) for us [taking paths which He prepared ahead of time], that we should walk in them [living the good life which He prearranged and made ready for us to live].

Ephesians 2:10 AMP

REFLECTIONS

What is an Ancient Pathway?

_____
_____
_____
_____
_____

What is God's Foreknowledge?

_____
_____
_____
_____
_____

JOURNAL YOUR THOUGHTS ON THIS CHAPTER

Chapter
Two

Roots and Origins

A while back my wife and I were guests in the beautiful home of one of our dear friends who pastors a thriving church in Tulsa, Oklahoma. She is a well-known national and international prophetess. We were sitting in her gorgeous kitchen talking about things pertaining to the Kingdom of God.

Suddenly, the presence of the Lord came upon her. She gave me that "prophetic bull's-eye look," which seemed to be saying: "Francis, God wants to talk to you, now!" She started to prophesy into my life. Here is part of the prophecy from the Spirit of God: *"God has called you to teach the Body of Christ roots and origins. Many people in the Body of Christ do not like roots and origins. But you do, says the Lord. God is going to use you to show the Body of Christ that if the roots and origins of something they are doing are satanic, they cannot make them godly, no matter what they do to them!"*

Unlike the scientific community, who believe that the answers to the world's problems are predicated on future technological and scientific breakthroughs; God's Kingdom operates on the premise that all the answers to today's problems (and the future), are found in rediscovering the ancient paths, that God wired into the fabric of creation eons of years ago. These ancient pathways are the general blueprints that govern all of God's creation. This leads us to one of my favorite subjects in Scripture: The Subject of Roots and Origins. Those who know me know that I am very passionate about roots and origins, and how they affect our God-given destiny as well as that of all of creation.

Defining Roots and Origins

Let us first begin this chapter by defining roots and origins. What are roots and origins? This is the billion-dollar question of this chapter. *Roots and origins are the foundational blueprints and principles, that God has embedded in the fabric of creation, that govern the past, present and future state of things.* Roots and origins have power over Sin, the devil, and the angelic order and over all of mankind. Nothing in creation is beyond the reach of roots and origins. A dear friend of mine, Prophet Kevin Leal, once made a profound statement about roots and origins that has never left my mind. He told me: "Francis, things don't end wrong, they start wrong!" I have come to respect the wisdom of this statement, in observing how the principle of roots and origins affects interpersonal relationships (especially in marriage and business relationships).

> *In the beginning was the Word, and the Word was with God, and the Word was God. The same was in the beginning with God. All things were made by him; and without him was not any thing made that was made.*
>
> John 1:1-3

John 1:1-3 is one of the most profound Scripture passages on the subject of roots and origins. This passage tells us that in the beginning was the Word. We know from Scripture that Christ Himself is the Word that was in the beginning with God. The Apostle John also tells us: "But all things where made by him (Christ) and without him (Christ) was not anything made that was made". This means that every credible law of the universe, man's DNA, and all forms of matter (whether visible or invisible), were created by Him and through Him. This also means that the best physicist, scientist or biochemist is the fellow who acknowledges the impact of Christ, on the tapestry of creation. To ignore Christ in creation, and his impact on all created material, is a colossal mistake and miscalculation.

The above passage, from the book of John, is not meant to be a negation of science and technology but rather the acknowledgment that Christ, the Word of the living God, is the raw material that God used to create all forms of matter within the universe. This is why I truly believe that this Kingdom Age is going to bring with it some of the greatest physicists, scientists and biochemists that the world has ever known. They will not be afraid to acknowledge the presence and impact of Christ on all created materials, both spiritual and natural. This new breed of global intellectuals is going to factor in Christ, as the root and origin of all of creation. If we then acknowledge that Christ is the raw material behind all created life forms, we also have to conclude that Christ created all DNA. We would then have to admit that Christ (God's living Word) is in every strand of DNA in our human genome.

His Divinity upon Our Humanity

Always bearing about in the body the dying of the Lord Jesus that the life also of Jesus might be made manifest in our body.
2 Corinthians 4:10 KJV

Since Christ is the raw material for all created life forms, including man's DNA, it follows then that Christ (the visible image of the invisible God), is the best solution to the healing of any medical or diabolical genetic mutation. Christ can reconfigure or reconstruct our DNA and fix any anomalies in our genetic sequence, by the supernatural imposition of His divinity upon our humanity. This book contains the prophetic architecture of how Christ's divinity, superimposed over our humanity, can help us break free of years of generational iniquity, and enter into a glorious inheritance.

Bringing the Future out of the Past

I know that, whatsoever God doeth, it shall be forever: nothing can be put to it, nor any thing taken from it: and God doeth it, that men should fear before him That which hath been is now; and that which is to be hath already been; and God requireth that which is past.
Ecclesiastes 3:14-15

Ecclesiastes 3:14-15 is one of my favorites Scripture passages on the dynamics of roots and origins. The writer of this passage of Scripture makes some very important statements that will help cement our understanding of roots and origins and how they affect the future destiny. Below is a brief summation of these powerful prophetic statements that King Solomon makes in the passage above.

King Solomon tells us that whatever God does is forever. This statement, by itself, tells us that if we want anything in our life to last, and be successful, we have to build it around what God is doing. This means that every action, which does not have the fingerprint of God in its roots and origins, will ultimately end in failure (or lead us into great frustration).

The expression *"and nothing can be added to it..."* in the passage above, leads us into the second important spiritual factor that governs roots and origins: Since roots and origins are based on God's foreknowledge, they are beyond demonic and human manipulation. There is absolutely nothing that we can do to improve on the quality of what God has already established, in the tapestry of creation. That is why the best genetic engineering cannot improve on what God established and wired into the human genome. The expression *"and nothing can be added to it..."* also explains why obedience is better than sacrifice to God.

The expression *"That which hath been is now; and that which is to be hath already been;"* in the passage above, leads us into this third important spiritual factor that governs roots and origins: *"There is absolutely nothing new under the Sun that God has not already done in His Son."* This statement also means that the devil has no fresh ideas to carry out his diabolical assignments in the earth that he has not already tried in the past. This also means that there is a powerful divine antidote to counteract every form of genetic mutation that is demonically engineered.

The expression *"God requireth that which is past..."* is probably one of the most important statements that King Solomon ever made about the subjects of roots and origins, and their inherent power over the present and future state of things. Human beings normally like to run away from their past, and believe that the best version of themselves is always in the future. But not so with God.

The question that quickly comes to mind is this *"Why would a God who knows the end from the beginning be so stuck on requiring the past from the present generation?"* The reason why most human beings do not like reflecting too much on the past is because more often than not we are the most ashamed of what we have done in the past; not so with God. There is nothing God has ever done in eternity-past that He is ashamed of. As a matter of Bible study, God's best work is not coming in a future time frame. God's best work is already done. Even Jesus Christ was in actuality the Lamb that was slain before the foundation of the world, even though it took us over 4000 years of human history to figure this out. In the corridors of eternity, Christ was already the *"lamb slain"* before God gave us a visible demonstration of that eternal reality on the cross.

Had Christ not been the Lamb of God, already slain in the corridors of eternity before He came to the earth, His sacrifice on the cross would have been of little value to us. This is because any sacrifice that originates out of the earth realm would have had a very short leash on its redemptive powers. Anything that is born within the cylinder of time and space is subject to both the power and limitations of time and space. If Christ's blood were of earthly origins, it would have been limited in its redemptive ability to intercept both heaven and earth with the benefits of redemption. From a genetic perspective, if Christ's blood was of earthly origins, it could not be used to heal the broken down genetics of the human race. In the next chapter, we will go into an in-depth study of the blood of Christ and how it provides us with an everlasting solution to our compromised genetics.

May Ishmael live under your Special Blessing

And I will bless her and give you a son from her! Yes, I will bless her richly, and she will become the mother of many nations. Kings of nations will be among her descendants." Then Abraham bowed down to the ground, but he laughed to himself in disbelief. "How could I become a father at the age of 100?" he thought. "And how can Sarah have a baby when she is ninety years old?" So Abraham said to God, "May Ishmael live under your special blessing!" But God replied, "No—Sarah, your wife, will give birth to a son for you.

You will name him Isaac, and I will confirm my covenant with him and his descendants as an everlasting covenant.

Genesis 17:16-19

We see the same powerful prophetic principal concerning spiritual roots and origins played out in a most revealing way, in the life of Abraham. God had made a covenant promise to Abraham, that he would give him a son through his wife Sarah. When God first gave this prophetic promise to Abraham and Sarah, it was much easier for them to believe it. They were both relatively young. Then, months turned into many years of waiting. Along the way, Sarah gave up the hope of becoming a mother in her old age. She devised a plan that was in actuality the kiss of death. Sarah decided to help God fulfill His covenant promise by telling Abraham to sleep with her Egyptian maid Hagar. Therefore, the child that Hagar would bear (as her servant) would be considered as if it was Sarah's child.

I imagine that Sarah did not have a difficult time selling her latest idea to her aging husband. How often does an old married man get the blessing of his wife to sleep with a beautiful 18-year-old maid? Abraham was probably in Hagar's tent long before Sarah could have second thoughts. From the outside, Sarah's plan looked brilliant. But, she and Abraham had walked into a demonic trap. They had made a monumental error that would haunt them for the rest of their lives.

So Abram had sexual relations with Hagar, and she became pregnant. But when Hagar knew she was pregnant, she began to treat her mistress, Sarai, with contempt.

> *Then Sarai said to Abram, "This is all your fault! I put my servant into your arms, but now that she's pregnant she treats me with contempt. The LORD will show who's wrong—you or me!"*
>
> Genesis 16:4-5

Like a rattlesnake forced into a corner, Sarah's brilliant plan quickly backfired and struck at the core of her marriage to Abraham. The son born through her Egyptian maid, whom she had thought would bring her great joy, only brought sorrow and death into her life. The ensuing spiritual tension caused Abraham and Sarah to begin to have marital problems and infighting. The true roots and origins of what they had created were paving a way for devils to attack them.

Sarah wondered why her sincere and "well-thought-out plan" to help God turned so terribly wrong. The answer is found in understating spiritual roots and origins. If something has its roots and origins in a satanic power play, there is little we can do to change the true nature of what the thing really is. Hagar's son, Ishmael, was born out of a spirit of self-will and rebellion to God's authority. There was no way this child could bring the fullness of joy and laughter which God had promised would come with the birth of Isaac. The spiritual roots and origins of Abraham's Ishmael went all the way back to the ten gods of Egypt, not to mention the devil himself, who was the principal spirit behind Egyptian idolatry.

When the appointed time came for God's Isaac to be born, Abraham had a difficult time releasing his faith because he was so enamored with the child that he had produced by his own power. Abraham actually interceded for Ishmael. He asked God to have Ishmael replace Isaac. God would not hear of it. God refused to hear of it because Abraham did not know the spiritual ramifications of what he was asking. He did not know that when something is built on demonic technology, its root system is established in hellish operations. No matter what God did to Ishmael he would have remained, at best, half divine and half devilish. Ishmael was a mixed blessing at best.

The Birth of Ishmael

> *Now Sarai, Abram's wife, had not been able to bear children for him. But she had an Egyptian servant named Hagar. So Sarai said to Abram, "The Lord has prevented me from having children. Go and sleep with my servant. Perhaps I can have children through her." And Abram agreed with Sarai's proposal.*
>
> Genesis 16:1-2

It is easy to see why Ishmael grew up to become a mixed blessing. When we examine the roots and origins of his birth we discover the reason for the breach in his birth. He was a child who was birthed by the engines of disobedience and unbelief by a woman who was so desperate for a child that she decided to help God fulfill His promise. Ishmael was a child who was therefore born with hybrid DNA. He was an attempt, by demonic powers, to usurp the birth of God's Isaac. Since the prophecy of the Messianic seed in Genesis chapter 3, the devil had been terrified of the birth of every man-child who was tied to a promise of God.

In the Genesis 3 prophecy, God told the Devil that he was placing enmity between God's seed in the womb of the woman and the devils seed. God promised in this ancient prophecy that His seed was going to crash the head of the serpent. Ever since God revealed His divine agenda of restoration, through the seed of the woman, the devil has taken particular interest in the birth of every man-child. Since this ancient prophecy the devil was determined to intercept the entrance of God's promised Messianic Seed. The best form of defense that the devil found, against the entrance of the Messianic seed, is to corrupt and infiltrate the genetics of every child born of a woman (in the hopes of defusing the power of God's Messianic seed). This is why Generational curses are also deeply insidious: They represent a passionate diabolical agenda, against the inherent destiny of God, inside every child born of a woman.

Since Ishmael was a born out of Sarah's despondence and unbelief, Ishmael's inherent genetics were already compromised by the spiritual technology surrounding his birth. This would explain why God refused to establish covenant with Ishmael, or include him in the earthly genealogy of Jesus Christ. The very name Ishmael means: "The wild one." Many of us are struggling in our spiritual walk because we are still carrying a "genetic make-up" that bears the imprint of "The wild one." This would explain why the apostle John, in his epistle, calls "Cain" of "The wicked one" even though by natural genealogy Cain was the firstborn son of Adam and Eve. Genetically, "Cain" was the son of the "wicked or wild one." The spiritual technology contained in this book is designed to help God-fearing children of God annihilate the "genetics of the wild one" within their genetic sequence.

The Birth of Isaac

The Lord kept his word and did for Sarah exactly what he had promised. She became pregnant, and she gave birth to a son for Abraham in his old age. This happened at just the time God had said it would. And Abraham named their son Isaac. Eight days after Isaac was born, Abraham circumcised him as God had commanded. Abraham was 100 years old when Isaac was born. And Sarah declared, "God has brought me laughter. All who hear about this will laugh with me. Who would have said to Abraham that Sarah would nurse a baby? Yet I have given Abraham a son in his old age!"

Genesis 21:1-6

On the other hand the birth of Isaac was based upon a more excellent spiritual technology and in complete compliance with God's predetermined purposes for the creation. Isaac was born as a result of God's foreknowledge. This essentially meant that for the most part his genetic imprint had a deeper godly imprint on it than that of Ishmael. This is not meant to suggest that Abraham's Isaac was born with the same perfect and flawless DNA that Yeshua was born with. But, he was a million miles more genetically superior to Ishmael. Isaac's genetic makeup was deeply embedded with a strong genetic leaning towards the fulfillment of God's predetermined counsel for the human race. This is why his birth released the spirit of joy in Abraham and Sarah's lives. The name "Isaac" literally means *"Laughter" (or) "The God who makes me laugh."* It is my prayer that the spiritual technology contained in this book will cause you to say: *"God has made me to laugh at the Generational Curses that used to challenge my forward advancement into my God given destiny."*

The War between Ishmael and Isaac

When Isaac grew up and was about to be weaned, Abraham prepared a huge feast to celebrate the occasion. But Sarah saw Ishmael—the son of Abraham and her Egyptian servant Hagar—making fun of her son, Isaac. So she turned to Abraham and demanded, "Get rid of that slave woman and her son. He is not going to share the inheritance with my son, Isaac. I won't have it!" This upset Abraham very much because Ishmael was his son. But God told Abraham, "Do not be upset over the boy and your servant. Do whatever Sarah tells you, for Isaac is the son through whom your descendants will be counted.

Genesis 21:8-11

Sarah's ill attempt to help God fulfill His prophetic promise through Hagar rapidly backfired like a cornered rattlesnake. As soon as Hagar became aware that she was pregnant with Abraham's baby her heart towards Sarah went through a rapid mutation. She began to look at Sarah with great contempt and began to fight for a bigger role in Abraham's life. The tension and strife between Sarah and Hagar quickly became palpable. It was a prophetic foreshadowing of the war that would eventually ensue between their lines of seed. The war between these two women in Abraham's household was also a foreshadowing of the ongoing war between the flesh and the spirit.

Immediately after the birth of Isaac, the Seed-wars reached a dangerous peak as it escalated from the "mothers" to their "children." The Bible says that when Abraham and Sarah put together a huge feast to celebrate the weaning of Isaac, their child of promise; Sarah observed Ishmael "the child of bondage" making mockery of Isaac. When Sarah saw this, she became very angry and told Abraham to cast Hagar and Ishmael out of their house. Sarah made it clear that they will be no sharing of the "Inheritance" between Abraham's Ishmael and Abraham's Isaac. Abraham was heartbroken over Sarah's request because he loved his son Ishmael. But God stepped into the middle of the "Seed-wars" and took Sarah's side. Abraham knew he was cornered when God took his wife's side on such a critical issue. But God was not really taking sides. He was simply protecting the ancient boundaries of His predetermined purposes for the human race. God knew that Ishmael's bloodline contained a mixture of Abraham's godly heritage and Hagar's demonically engineered Egyptian heritage. Ishmael was truly a "mixed blessing."

Seed Wars between Sonship DNA and Demonic Hybrid DNA

God told the serpent: "Because you've done this, you're cursed, cursed beyond all cattle and wild animals, Cursed to slink on your belly and eat dirt all your life. I'm declaring war between you and the Woman, between your offspring and hers.

He'll wound your head, you'll wound his heel."

Genesis 3:14-15 (The Message Bible)

From the closure of the gates (of the Garden of Eden) to the opening of the gates (of the New Jerusalem), the history of what we call "spiritual warfare" is the history of "Seed Wars" between God's seed and the devil's seed. At the consummation of the ages in Christ Jesus, God's providence will conclude these "Seed Wars" by the total annihilation of the devil and his offspring in the Lake of Fire that burns with fire and brimstone. *Then the devil, who had deceived them, was thrown into the fiery lake of burning sulfur, joining the beast and the false prophet. There they will be tormented day and night forever and ever (Revelation 20:10).* Until then, these "Seed

Wars" between mans prophetic Sonship DNA, and the demonic hybrid DNA (man's corrupted gene pool) will rage on. But God has an everlasting and present day remedy for citizens of the Kingdom of God, who desire to live above the dictates of the demonic technology in their own genetics. This book contains the solution to this ancient battle between good and evil within our person.

> *Therefore, since we are surrounded by such a huge crowd of witnesses to the life of faith, let us strip off every weight that slows us down, especially the sin that so easily trips us up. And let us run with endurance the race God has set before us. We do this by keeping our eyes on Jesus, the champion who initiates and perfects our faith. Because of the joy awaiting him, he endured the cross, disregarding its shame. Now he is seated in the place of honor beside God's throne. Think of all the hostility he endured from sinful people; then you won't become weary and give up. After all, you have not yet given your lives in your struggle against sin.*
>
> Hebrews 12:1-4

The above passage contains a thrilling story of Christ's ultimate triumph over the "Seed Wars" but it also contains the best description of Generational Curses. In Hebrews 12:1 the apostle Paul admonishes believers to "strip themselves" of the "weights that slows them down, and the habitual sins that so easily trips them up." Based upon this premise, *"Generational Curses"* are simply *"demonically engineered weights or baggage. They are genetically embedded sinful responses that constantly get the best of us even when we desire to do right."* But, we are commanded to run with patience the race that God has set before us.

The apostle Paul tells us in Hebrews 12:4 that Christ Himself was not exempt from the impact of these "Seed Wars" between good and evil. The writer of Hebrews shows us that "Christ" (who represents the truest essence of "Sonship DNA") endured great contradictions against His person from religious zealots. They pretended to be the children of Abraham but manifested the genetic behavior of the bloodline of the "wild one." This historical fight between Jesus Christ and the religious zealots of His day foreshadows the ongoing internal warfare between good and evil from within our genetic make up. This genetic disturbance can explain why many born again believers desire to do what is right and then end up doing the exact opposite. These internal "Seed Wars" can explain why many children of God contradict their own convictions and violate the leading of the Holy Spirit (then hate themselves for doing so). But, do not despair; this book contains the divine antidote that will cause you to experience "Genetic Salvation."

LIFE APPLICATION SECTION

MEMORY VERSE

Therefore, since we are surrounded by such a huge crowd of witnesses to the life of faith, let us strip off every weight that slows us down, especially the sin that so easily trips us up. And let us run with endurance the race God has set before us. We do this by keeping our eyes on Jesus, the champion who initiates and perfects our faith. Because of the joy awaiting him, he endured the cross, disregarding its shame. Now he is seated in the place of honor beside God's throne. Think of all the hostility he endured from sinful people; then you won't become weary and give up. After all, you have not yet given your lives in your struggle against sin.

Hebrews 12:1-4

REFLECTIONS

What are Roots and Origins?

_____
_____
_____
_____
_____

What are Seed Wars?

_____
_____
_____
_____
_____

JOURNAL YOUR THOUGHTS ON THIS CHAPTER

Chapter Three

Man's Original Prophetic DNA

When I was working on this book the Holy Spirit gave me a stunning revelation. The Lord knows that Amos 3:7 is one of my favorite scriptures in the Bible. This passage of scripture says *"the Lord God does nothing without revealing His secrets to His servants the prophets."* The Holy Spirit told me that Amos 3:7 would not have applied to Adam and Eve before they fell from grace. The Holy Spirit also told me that Adam and Eve did not need external stimuli such as prophecy or preaching to help them walk out the plan of God for their lives.

The Holy Spirit then told me that when God created Adam and Eve, He gave them perfect Sonship DNA. Every prophetic instruction or prophecy concerning their future destiny or ambassadorial assignments within the earth realm was deeply embedded in their DNA. Adam and Eve had the same type of prophetic or Sonship DNA that the Lord Jesus Christ had while He was on earth. The testimony of prophecy was inherently present in their genetic make-up. Their genetic configuration contained the prophecy of things to come. Armed with this understanding let us examine Genesis 1:26-28.

> *Then God said, "Let us make human beings in our image, to be like us. They will reign over the fish in the sea, the birds in the sky, the livestock, all the wild animals on the earth, and the small animals that scurry along the ground." So God created human beings in his own image. In the image of God he created them; male and female he created them. Then God blessed them and said, "Be fruitful and multiply. Fill the earth and govern it. Reign over the fish in the sea, the birds in the sky, and all the animals that scurry along the ground."*
>
> Genesis 1:26-28

The Holy Spirit challenged me to take another look at this passage from the book of Genesis and examine it from a genetic standpoint. When God said, *"let us make man in our image and likeness;"* God's image and likeness was also deeply embedded or imprinted onto man's genetic makeup. It was not just Adam's spirit and soul that were created in the image and likeness of God. Consider for instance that when God blessed man and pronounced the following blessing: *"Be fruitful and multiply. Fill the earth and govern it. Reign over the fish in the sea, the birds in the sky, and all the animals that scurry along the ground"*...God was actually wiring and imprinting the ability to be fruitful and multiply as well as the ability to govern the earth and subdue it onto man's DNA.

This means that God's dominion mandate was superimposed by God's creative power on Adam's spirit and on his genetics. Imagine this: Every strand of DNA in Adam and Eve's DNA bore the imprint of Genesis 1:28 (Their ambassadorial assignment to advance the Kingdom of God by making earth a colony of the heavenly Kingdom was deeply embedded in their genetics). Since they had perfect DNA, they knew instinctively what they were born to do. This inherent genetic knowledge, of their prophetic calling to rule the creation here on earth, did not violate their ability to exercise freewill.

The Tree of the Knowledge of Good and Evil

The Lord God placed the man in the Garden of Eden to tend and watch over it. But the Lord God warned him, "You may freely eat the fruit of every tree in the garden—except the tree of the knowledge of good and evil. If you eat its fruit, you are sure to die."

Genesis 2:15

After God created Adam the Bible says that God placed the first Kingdom Ambassador in the Garden of Eden to tend and watch over it. By all accounts, this garden was a reservoir of divine abundance. There was absolutely nothing missing or broken in this garden, it was as perfect as the Kingdom it represented. Inside the enclosure of this garden Adam and Eve lacked for nothing. But their continued residency in the garden of abundance was predicated on obeying one simple instruction from God: There was a Tree of the knowledge of good and evil that God told them they were not to eat of. He said that in the day that they ate of the Tree of the knowledge of good and evil, they would die. Unfortunately, we all know how this story ended.

Adam and Eve were visited by the devil who was masquerading as a talking serpent. Under this guise, the enemy of our souls managed to cause Adam and Eve to doubt the integrity of God's word. He caused the first Kingdom Ambassadors to commit high treason. After they ate of the forbidden fruit, they became overpowered by an entity called "Sin" (and its insidious powers). This entity called "Sin" introduced death agencies into man's bloodline and genetic makeup. The pure prophetic DNA that God had given to Adam and Eve became breached by the entrance of death agencies. The entrance of these death agencies, in Adam's bloodline, led to the most catastrophic demonic genetic mutation ever known to mankind.

Wrestling with Genetic Bondage

I want to do what is good, but I don't. I don't want to do what is wrong, but I do it anyway. But if I do what I don't want to do, I am not really the one doing wrong; it is sin living in me that does it. I have discovered this principle of life—that when I want to do what is right, I inevitably do what is wrong. I love God's law with all my heart. But there is another power within me that is at war with my mind. This power makes me a slave to the sin that is still within me.

Romans 7:19-23

Without a doubt, one of the greatest apostles who have ever lived is the apostle Paul. But the apostle Paul was no stranger to the inherent power of genetic bondage. Paul tells us that he desired to do what is good but ended up doing the very things he hated doing. This passage suggests that the wrestling that the apostle Paul is alluding to in this passage of Scripture is not the mental struggle against sin. It is something far much most sinister and powerful. What the apostle Paul is describing, in the above passage of Scripture, is a war between good and evil that takes place in every human being on a genetic level. My dear friend, there is no spiritual bondage more sinister and more controlling than the bondage that manifests itself on the genetic level. This is because genetic bondage has the power to weave its insidious nature into our personality profile to such an extent that we will find ourselves defending unrighteousness behavior by saying that it is just who we are.

In his fight to do what was right and righteous, the apostle Paul discovered to his utter dismay that there was a principle of sin that was operating in the very crevices of his DNA. What's more, the apostle Paul was the first one to acknowledge that his mental fortitude and spiritual passion to do what is right was no match against the pull of evil within his genetics. The apostle Paul discovered that he was more of a slave to sin on the genetic level than he was on the mental level. But, thank God that the cry of the apostle Paul did not end in total despair but in the uncovering of God's remedy to his genetic struggle and anomalies. Paul's cry for deliverance from this insidious genetic bondage ends with the following proclamation:

> *Oh, what a miserable person I am! Who will free me from this life that is dominated by sin and death? Thank God! The answer is in Jesus Christ our Lord. So you see how it is: In my mind I really want to obey God's law, but because of my sinful nature I am a slave to sin.*
>
> Romans 7:24-25

The Last Adam

So also it is written, the first man Adam became a living soul. The last Adam became a life-giving spirit.

1 Corinthians 15:45 KJV

The Bible tells us: The Lord Jesus Christ came to us through the virgin birth in order to cancel, overturn and overthrow every diabolical spirit and entity that the first Adam brought into our world, when he sinned against God. The Bible calls "Christ" the "Last Adam" who is also a *life-giving spirit*. The Lord Jesus Christ is called the "Last Adam" because: There is no other "man" coming through the portals of time and space that can overturn and override everything that the first Adam unleashed (Into the portals of time and space through his act of rebellion).

Since the Lord Jesus Christ is the last Adam, He is the only divine antidote for the healing of all types of genetic anomalies ushered into our *"ration of genes"* by the sin of the first man, Adam. *This would explain why God Almighty went to great lengths to make sure that the birth of Christ was not only supernatural but also genetically accurate.* Had Jesus Christ's genetics been compromised during His birth, He would hold no answers or remedies for those of us who are fighting deeply entrenched spiritual and emotional genetic bondages. Let us now examine the supernatural birth of Yeshua (Jesus), so we can see how God ensured genetic purity in the birth of Yeshua (Jesus).

The Virgin Birth

"Don't be afraid, Mary," the angel told her, "for you have found favor with God! You will conceive and give birth to a son, and you will name him Jesus. He will be very great and will be called the Son of the Most High. The Lord God will give him the throne of his ancestor David. And he will reign over Israel forever; his Kingdom will never end!" Mary asked the angel, "But how can this happen? I am a virgin." The angel replied, "The Holy Spirit will come upon you, and the power of the Most High will overshadow you. So the baby to be born will be holy, and he will be called the Son of God.

Luke 1:30-35

The prophet Isaiah, who lived about 700 BC, gave a prophetic message to the nation of Israel that I believe many of his countrymen found hard to believe. He told the people that God would give them a very unusual "Prophetic Sign" that a virgin in Israel would be found pregnant with a child implanted in her womb by God Himself. Scientifically, it is impossible for a virgin to be with child without a male sperm donor.

True to His word through the prophet Isaiah, in the *fullness of times*, God sent His highest-ranking angel, in the form of the angel Gabriel, to deliver Isaiah's ancient prophecy. After the angel finished his salutations and telling young Mary that she was about to be the mother of a son, the perplexed girl asked the most important question of the whole divine encounter: *"How can I become pregnant without sleeping with a man?"* The angel Gabriel told her that the power of the Highest would overshadow her womb and supernaturally implant "Christ" the man-child into her womb.

The billion-dollar question is why would God bring up such an unusual pregnancy?

Advancements in biology underscore God's genius behind the virgin birth of the Last Adam. *According to biologists, once the fetus is implanted in the mother's womb, the Mothers blood (under normal body conditions) NEVER comes in direct contact with the developing baby.* The mother's blood supplies nutrients to the placenta, which transfers nutrients and oxygen to the baby's blood. This explains why God used the womb of a virgin to bring into our world God's masterpiece, the man "Christ Jesus." Yeshua was God's perfect man with zero genetic anomalies or deficiencies. He represented the perfect humanity.

The acts of sexual intercourse between a man and a woman, or the implantation of a man's sperm into a woman's egg, were both completely excluded during the supernatural virgin birth of Christ. Since Yeshua's fetus was not a by-product of the chemical combination of Joseph's sperm and Mary's egg, Yeshua (Jesus) did not acquire His "ration of Genes" from either Mary or Joseph. Since Yeshua's ration of Genes did not originate from His earthly parents, where did they come from? Yeshua's (Jesus) "ration of Genes" came directly from the throne of God. God created Yeshua's "ration of Genes" out of the heavens just like He had created Adam's. The first and the last Adam are the only two people in recorded human history whose ration of Genes was not earthly but heavenly. This is why the Bible refers to the first Adam as "Adam, the Son of God."

Yeshua: The Perfect Man

Said unto them, Ye have brought this man unto me, as one that perverteth the people: and, behold, I, having examined him before you, have found no fault in this man touching those things whereof ye accuse him:

Luke 23:14 KJV

After the fall of Adam, the first man, every human being who has been born into the world was born spiritually, emotionally, genetically and physically broken. This would quickly explain why God could not raise a "Savior" for mankind from within our own ranks. God had to outsource our salvation and redemption to a different and special kind of man, a perfect man without any blemish in His spirit or body.

Since a perfect man, without any inherent blemishes in his total being could not be found within our ranks, God was compelled to look to Himself to find such man. Man was created as a triune being. That means that he is a spirit being who posses a soul and is housed in a physical body. God had to find a man who could bear the imprint of complete perfection in all three areas. Thus, Christ stepped out of the portals of eternity, and stepped into an incorruptible body created by His Father in heaven.

For it is not possible that the blood of bulls and of goats should take away sins.5 Wherefore when he cometh into the world, he saith, Sacrifice and offering thou wouldest not, but a body hast thou prepared me:

Hebrews 10:4-5 KJV

Just like God went to the dust of the ground to create Adam's body, *God supernaturally created Christ's body.* If this is the case, then Jesus Christ's body was perfect in its genetic, structural and biological composition. We have already given evidence of the fact that Yeshua's blood and His "ration of Genes" came from the throne room of God. The Combination of all of these factors, in one man, simply certifies the fact that Yeshua was truly the *"Perfect Specimen"* of a man without any form of blemish.

This fact alone is sufficient to open a portal of hope for every member of the human race who is wrestling with Generational curses and genetic anomalies.

The Precious Blood of Christ

The blood of Jesus Christ is truly the most precious blood in the canals of human history. In the world of precious minerals, any mineral that is very rare to find is considered priceless. The more rare a mineral is, the more value it has. Following this reasoning, the blood of Jesus Christ is the most precious bloodline in creation because it contains the DNA of God. The blood of Christ represents a flawless and an uncorrupted bloodline. This means that the genetic pool of the blood of Jesus Christ contains the best specimen of DNA. Scientists in the field of stem cell research would be overjoyed if they ever got an uncontaminated sample of Christ's DNA. This is because they know that they could heal so many diseases that are genetically induced, if they could medicate their patients with the high quality DNA taken from a flawless gene pool.

We have already mentioned the fact that during the supernatural birth of Jesus Christ through the virgin birth, Yeshua (Jesus) did not share in His mother's bloodline. *Had Christ's blood been mixed with Mary's blood, Mary's sin ravaged bloodline would have corrupted the flawless genetic gene pool that was inherent in Christ's blood.* Had this happened, any chances we had for a supernatural blood transfusion would have been lost. Medical doctors who oversee any hospital's blood bank know that the purer the blood sample, the better it is for the patient who is receiving the blood transfusion. If the donor's blood is infected with the HIV virus, and this blood sample is injected into any patient, the patient will immediately become infected with the HIV virus.

This is why nurses and medical doctors, who use donated blood samples from the blood bank, take the blood samples through a very thorough blood analysis, to make sure that the blood that is being transfused into any patient will not complicate the patient's condition. God in His eternal genius knew just how valuable the blood of Christ would be to millions of lost souls with sin ravaged bloodlines. Just to give you a graphic picture of just how valuable and priceless the blood of Jesus Christ is to fallen humanity, let us imagine for the moment that we are on a desert. On this desert, there is a severe shortage of water and one thousand desperately thirsty adults who are willing to kill for a bottle of drinking water. Let us now suppose that there are only one hundred water bottles on the entire desert Island. What kind of desperate fight for survival do you think would ensue among the population of one thousand adults? If you can imagine this scenario, then you are beginning to scratch the tip of the iceberg, concerning the preciousness of the blood of Christ to our fallen humanity. Let us suppose that you are a patient infected with AIDS and the best doctors have described your case as terminal. Let us now suppose that while you are hanging on to dear life, one of your best friends dashes into your hospital room and makes a stunning announcement.

Your friend says: *"The doctors have found a man with perfect DNA. The doctors are so excited about this man. They are saying that this man's blood is so pure and so potent that they believe one drop of his blood can instantly heal anyone with full-blown AIDS."* How would you feel at the news of the discovery of such a man? Especially, when you know that you will be at the receiving end of the awesome benefits of taking one drop of his blood into your system. I believe you would be completely ecstatic. Your joy at the existence of such a man would not know any bounds.

Genetic Salvation

Thank you for allowing me the opportunity to excite your God given imagination. The reality is that the analogies that I have used are based on reality. Since the fall of Adam and Eve, all of mankind was forced into a spiritual desert, starved of the living waters of the Kingdom of God. Secondarily, every man and woman within creation is under the penalty of sin and is infected with spiritual full-blown AIDS. From a prophetic standpoint, all of humanity is trapped in the hospital room of our sinful condition awaiting the sentence of eternal destruction. But, one day over two thousand years ago, a badly beaten Jewish Rabbi died on a cross. He shed His precious blood on that cross to quench our spiritual thirst and to heal us from the spiritual AIDS virus that runs rampart in our sinful nature.

The Holy Spirit gave me a stunning revelation when I was working on this book: "Breaking Generational Curses under the Order of Melchizedek." He said to me: *"Son, many of my people are truly born again, but many have not yet experienced genetic salvation."* I had never heard of the expression "Genetic Salvation." I was born again over two decades ago. The Holy Spirit showed me that the Lord Jesus Christ truly redeemed the whole man: *spirit, soul and body*. But, how many of us are truly experiencing the *"Genetic Salvation"* that Jesus Christ purchased for us? The Lord told me that *"Genetic Salvation"* occurs when we apply, by faith, the finished work of Christ to our broken down genetics (so that we can inherit Christ's Sonship DNA). *Christ's Sonship DNA will help us to obey the Gospel of the Kingdom and walk in righteousness on a genetic level.* Achieving the fore-mentioned condition is the essence of this writing.

LIFE APPLICATION SECTION

MEMORY VERSE

Then God said, "Let us make human beings in our image, to be like us. They will reign over the fish in the sea, the birds in the sky, the livestock, all the wild animals on the earth, and the small animals that scurry along the ground." So God created human beings in his own image. In the image of God he created them; male and female he created them. Then God blessed them and said, "Be fruitful and multiply. Fill the earth and govern it. Reign over the fish in the sea, the birds in the sky, and all the animals that scurry along the ground."

Genesis 1:26-28

REFLECTIONS

What is Prophetic DNA?

_____
_____
_____
_____
_____

What is Genetic Bondage?

_____
_____
_____
_____
_____

JOURNAL YOUR THOUGHTS ON THIS CHAPTER

Chapter

Four

Demonic Genetic Mutation

In this chapter we will take a deep introspective look at a spiritual and scientific phenomenon known as "Genetic Mutation." We will first define genetic mutation from a scientific point of view.

A Scientific Definition

At a basic level, mutation causes a gene or genetic sequence to change from its original or intended purpose. It can be caused by a variety of internal or external sources, and the side effects can be positive or negative for the organism that undergoes mutation.

> *This is the book of the generations of Adam. In the day that God created man, in the likeness of God made he him; Male and female created he them; and blessed them, and called their name Adam, in the day when they were created. And Adam lived an hundred and thirty years, and begat a son in his own likeness, and after his image; and called his name Seth:*
>
> Genesis 5:1-3

Genesis 5:1-3 contains the account of the saddest genetic mutation in human history. I really believe that heaven wept over this unfortunate transition in man's genetic makeup. This passage bears record to the worst and fastest genetic degeneration in recorded human history. In Genesis 5:1 the Bible tells us that Adam and Eve (male and female) were created in God's likeness. They carried the imprint of God's likeness on their genetics. They both had the DNA of God flowing through their veins. They were the perfect specimens of humans. They had a prophetic DNA or Sonship DNA that governed their personality profile, internal motivations and personal destiny. Unfortunately this state of things was not to last, because an ensuing demonic cloud of deception was already beginning to cast a black shadow over their inheritance. God had given them a stern warning that on the day that they ate of the Tree of the knowledge of good and evil, they would be inviting the technology of death into their lives.

God's warning proved immutable, after they committed the treasonous offense of following the voice of an unemployed Cherub masquerading as a talking serpent who encroached upon their legal territory. Unfortunately they heeded the devil's lie and ate of the forbidden fruit. True to God's Word *"Sin and the death agencies that it brings rushed into their spirit, soul and body."* When these death agencies entered man's previously pure bloodline; they created great chaos in man's genetic sequence. These Sin driven chaotic movements, in man's genetic composition, broke down the imprint of God's likeness off the template of the human genome leaving several gaps within man's genetic sequence. These gaps created in man's genetic sequence by "Sin's" chaotic infringement of man's DNA were quickly filled with demonic spirits and demonic technologies. Scientists tell us that one genetic letter or Chromosome out of its proper genetic sequence can be responsible for causing life threatening diseases like the ones listed below.

Cystic fibrosis *(also known as* **CF** *or* **mucoviscidosis***) is a common disease which affects the entire body, causing progressive disability and often early death. The name cystic fibrosis refers to the characteristic scarring and cyst formation within the pancreas, first recognized in the 1930s. Difficulty breathing is the most serious symptom and results from frequent lung infections that are treated, though not cured, by antibiotics and other medications. A multitude of other symptoms, including sinus infections, poor growth, diarrhea, and infertility result from the effects of CF on other parts of the body. CF is caused by a mutation in the gene for the protein cystic fibrosis transmembrane conductance regulator* (CFTR). *This gene is required to regulate the components of sweat, digestive juices, and mucus.*

Down syndrome, *or* **Down's syndrome trisomy 21,** *or* **trisomy G,** *is a chromosomal disorder caused by the presence of all or part of an extra 21st chromosome. It is named after John Langdon Down, the physician who described the syndrome in 1866. The disorder was identified as a chromosome 21 trisomy by Jérôme Lejeune in 1959. The condition is characterized by a combination of major and minor differences in structure. Down syndrome in a fetus can be identified with amniocentesis during pregnancy or in a baby at birth.*

Demonic Genetic Mutation

Duchenne muscular dystrophy (DMD) *is a severe recessive X-linked form of muscular dystrophy characterized by rapid progression of muscle degeneration, eventually leading to loss of ambulation and death. This affliction affects one in 3500 males, making it the most prevalent of muscular dystrophies. In general, only males are afflicted, though females can be carriers. Females may be afflicted if the father is afflicted and the mother is also a carrier/affected. The disorder is caused by a mutation in the dystrophin gene, located in humans on the* X *chromosome (Xp21). The dystrophin gene codes for the protein dystrophin, an important structural component within muscle tissue. Dystrophin provides structural stability to the* dystroglycan complex (DGC), *located on the cell membrane. (Articles taken From Wikipedia, the free encyclopedia)*

Demonically Engineered Genetic Mutation

Then the people began to multiply on the earth, and daughters were born to them. The sons of God saw the beautiful women and took any they wanted as their wives. Then the Lord said, "My Spirit will not put up with humans for such a long time, for they are only mortal flesh. In the future, their normal lifespan will be no more than 120 years." In those days, and for some time after, giant Nephilites lived on the earth, for whenever the sons of God had intercourse with women, they gave birth to children who became the heroes and famous warriors of ancient times.

Genesis 6:1-4

We finally get to the place where we can now discuss demonically engineered genetic mutation on a much deeper level. *The sixth chapter of Genesis contains the nomenclature of all demonically engineered genetic mutation.* The Bible tells us that when men began to multiply on the earth and daughters were born to them; fallen Angels took notice of the beauty of the daughters of men. The beauty of the daughters of men excited the engines of lust within these fallen Angels. Besides the pure sexual lust that these fallen Angels had for the daughters of men, their interest in the daughters of men was also deeply driven by the devil's diabolical conspiracy to destroy and defile the entrance of the Messianic seed into the human race.

Like a fugitive on the run from the Law, the devil was terrified of the entrance of the promised Messianic seed that was destined to crash the head of the serpent. Since God had made it very clear that this *promised violent seed of the Kingdom* would come through the womb of the woman, the devil put everywoman on earth under demonic surveillance. This demonic surveillance against the seed of the woman is the reason why so many women are oppressed and marginalized in most nations. Satan has from antiquity been deeply terrified of what comes out of the *"womb of the woman."* But in Genesis chapter six the devil devised a very diabolical plan that he thought would guarantee the total corruption of the entire human bloodline. The devils' plan involved inciting his coalition of fallen Angels to masquerade as men and begin to marry the daughters of men.

The sexual union between these fallen Angels and the daughters of men created a dangerous demonically engineered hybrid offspring. The offspring that resulted from these sexual unions between the daughters of men and these fallen Angels produced an offspring of giants in the earth. This race of giants was inherently wicked and violent. These giants known as Nephilims (in the Hebrew language) were so prone to violence that God even repented of having created mankind; because the whole earth was now full of violence and gross sexual immorality.

The demonic mutation that had transpired when the daughters of men were given in marriage to fallen Angels could be clearly evidenced in the physical appearance of the Nephilims. The Nephilims where gigantic in stature and many of them had six toes and six fingers. From the beginning of the creation God had never created a man with six fingers and toes. The Nephilims were therefore an abomination in nature. They were truly the freaks of nature. The Nephilims also grew at a very rapid rate. *Their genetic template was not only wicked, but also genetically superior to that of the average human being. The rate of genetic duplication and replication inside the genetics of the Nephilims could have baffled the greatest genetic scientists of our time.* But since the genetic mutation inside the genome of the Nephilims was demonically engineered to intercept the entrance of God's holy seed, none of the Nephilims mentioned in Scripture had a righteous inclination. They were true sons of hell. They brought the atmosphere and powers of hell wherever they went.

The Nephilims, though greatly diminished in number after the flood of Noah, continued to exist even to the days of King David. When his father Jesse sent David, to take cheese and bread to his brothers who were at the battlefront, he was greeted by the taunting voice of one of the few surviving Nephilims. His name was Goliath of Gath, a City of Philistia known for its idolatry, debauchery and immorality. The Bible tells us that for 40 days Goliath, the Philistine giant, was taunting the armies of Israel to send a man of war who could challenge him in a fight to the death contest. No one in the entire Israeli army dared to challenge this daunting sight of a man in a face-to-face Mortal Combat. No one dared to answer the menacing giant until David walked into the camp. David on the other hand was not afraid of the Giant's physical stature. David believed that this giant was no match for the power of God that had caused him to kill a Bear and a Lion with his bare hands. We all know how this story ended and how it canonized the name and fame of David into the corridors of human history. Goliath walked out toward David with his shield bearer ahead of him, 42 sneering in contempt at this ruddy-faced boy. 43 "Am I a dog," he roared at David, "that you come at me with a stick?" And he cursed David by the names of his gods. 44 "Come over here, and I'll give your flesh to the birds and wild animals!" *Goliath walked out toward David with his shield bearer ahead of him, 42 sneering in contempt at this ruddy-faced boy. 43 "Am I a dog," he roared at David, "that you come at me with a stick?" And he cursed David by the names of his gods. 44 "Come over here, and I'll give your flesh to the birds and wild animals!" Goliath yelled. 45 David replied to the Philistine, "You come to me with sword, spear, and javelin, but I come to you in the name of the Lord of Heaven's Armies—the God of the armies of Israel, whom you have defied. 48 As Goliath moved closer to attack, David quickly ran out to meet him. 49 Reaching into his shepherd's bag and taking out a stone, he hurled it with his sling and hit the Philistine in the forehead. The stone sank in, and Goliath stumbled and fell face down on the ground. 50 So David triumphed over the Philistine with only a sling and a stone, for he had no sword. 51 Then David ran over and pulled Goliath's sword from its sheath. David used it to kill him and cut off his head (1 Samuel 17).* The point I wanted to show you, from my re-enactment of David's fight with Goliath, is to show you that wherever you found any member of the Nephilims, they were always on the side of evil. They had no moral compass or genetic inclination towards anything righteous or godly. They were messengers of evil at all times and defiantly opposed to that which is holy. They truly had the imprint of their father the devil on their genetics.

The Nephilim Agenda

The Lord observed the extent of human wickedness on the earth, and he saw that everything they thought or imagined was consistently and totally evil. So the Lord was sorry he had ever made them and put them on the earth. It broke his heart. And the Lord said, "I will wipe this human race I have created from the face of the earth. Yes, and I will destroy every living thing—all the people, the large animals, the small animals that scurry along the ground, and even the birds of the sky. I am sorry I ever made them." But Noah found favor with the Lord.

Genesis 6:5-8

The devil's plan to destroy and infiltrate man's DNA and bloodline, so as to destroy the entrance of God's holy seed into the earth, is what is known as the "Nephilim agenda." A dear friend of mine by the name of Randy Demain (Kingdom Revelation Ministries; Austin, TX) has written a very powerful book on the subject called the *Nephilim Agenda*. It was published by XPMedia. I highly recommend this book to those of you who are interested in understanding the Nephilim agenda in greater detail. But it suffices to say that the primary reason God sent the flood, in the days of Noah, was to annihilate the Nephilim agenda that was spreading like wildfire on the earth. Before I understood the Nephilim agenda, I thought that God was very harsh in wiping out an entire race of people through a flood. But, I now know that the flood that God sent to destroy the world that Noah lived in was nothing short of the mercy of God. Through the Nephilim agenda, the devil intended to demonize and pervert the entire human race. Had he succeeded, God's plan of redemption would have been spoiled. The devil meant to erase the fingerprint of God on man's genetics and replace them with a genetic template of devils.

The phenomenon known as *Generational Curses* operates on the same demonic template as the Nephilim agenda; except that *Generational Curses* are better disguised. But, through the demonic technology called *Generational Curses*, we are reminded constantly that the devil has not given up on the Nephilim agenda. He still desires to plant his demonic DNA onto the human genome. The devil's primary desire has always been to take the place of God over the creation by controlling man. Controlling man is at the center of this demonic insurrection.

Same Sex Attraction

At the expense of being found guilty, of not being politically correct, I want to talk about another very common demonic genetic mutation. This demonic genetic mutation has widely become a global cultural and social phenomenon in the form of the gay lifestyle. The proponents of the gay lifestyle are "homosexuals" and "lesbians." By definition, a "homosexual" is a man who is sexually attracted to another man, in the same way that a heterosexual man is attracted to a woman. Conversely, a "lesbian" is a woman who is sexually attracted to another woman, in the same way that a heterosexual woman is attracted to a man.

I am not homophobic in any form or fashion. In God's sight, someone who struggles with the sin of lying is no different than a man who has sex with other men. They are both prisoners of the entity called "Sin." But, the global church makes a colossal mistake in simply dismissing the cultural and social phenomenon of same sex attraction into the sin column. What I am about to say might shock some conservative believers but, *"same sex attraction is not a sin. It is a demonically engineered demonic mutation within the human genome."* Same sex attraction only becomes sinful before God when the person so challenged begins to willfully act out their attraction, by having sex with persons of the same sex either mentally or physically.

God and the Science of Same Sex Attraction

Another colossal mistake that the global Church has made, in dealing with people who are trapped in the gay lifestyle is to quickly repudiate or deny the genetic science behind the phenomenon of same-sex attraction. From antiquity to the present times there has always been an uneasy tension between faith and science. But, this unfortunate tension has existed primarily because the Church itself has not experienced the "Intelligence of God," which is not intimidated in the face of scientific data. The Intelligence of God can meet science face-to-face and yet transcend the limitations of science.

I believe the scientists who now claim that same sex attraction is a normal genetically induced behavior (in the same way that heterosexual attraction to members of the opposite sex is a natural genetically induced behavior). Most church leaders get very uncomfortable and defensive in the face of such scientific conclusions. But, I personally believe that members of the scientific community, who claim that same sex attraction is a natural genetically induced behavior, are telling the truth based upon their own findings (even though some cases of homosexual behavior were induced by an act of sexual violation during childhood, by an adult person of the same or opposite sex). But, the colossal error of members of the scientific community, who support same sex attraction, lies in the fact that their scientific Data fails to account for the fact that the God, who created DNA, is capable of healing any genetic mutation that produces unnatural behavior, in the creation that contradicts the eternal Counsel of His Word.

Offering God's remedy to all forms of *"Generational Curses and Genetic Anomalies"* is what this book is all about.

Divine Refutation of Sinful Same Sex Attraction

If the global phenomenon of same sex attraction was a normal genetically induced behavior; we would expect this behavior to have both precedence and divine approval on it throughout the progressive revelation of the Holy Scriptures. Secondarily, we would also expect to find the practice of same-sex sexual unions within the relational matrix of lower forms of life in nature itself. But alas, even in nature among lower forms of life, the practice of same-sex sexual unions is sadly lacking. When we observe nature, what we see in great abundance is the phenomenon of "heterosexual unions." We see the sexual union of male and female lions; male and female monkeys; male and female birds; male and female dogs and the list is endless. Consider what God told Noah on how to transport every animal species into the future before the great flood:

> *Bring a pair of every kind of animal—a male and a female—into the boat with you to keep them alive during the flood. Pairs of every kind of bird, and every kind of animal, and every kind of small animal that scurries along the ground, will come to you to be kept alive.*
>
> Genesis 6:19-20

God gave Noah explicit instructions to carry male and female pairs of each animal species into the future. If you were given a tour of Noah's massive cruise liner, you would have been confronted with God's order for the creation. Each male caged animal in Noah's boat was caged with its female counterpart. This is the order of things that God chose for the New World after the flood. This order was not new. Because, in the beginning, this is the same order that God established, when the Scriptures declare that He created them male and female.

Let us look at some more scriptures from the Bible that can affirm that God does not consider same-sex sexual union as a normal expression of the DNA that He gave to mankind when we were created:

> *That evening the two angels came to the entrance of the city of Sodom. Lot was sitting there, and when he saw them, he stood up to meet them. Then he welcomed them and bowed with his face to the ground. "My lords," he said, "come to my home to wash your feet, and be my guests for the night. You may then get up early in the morning and be on your way again." "Oh no," they replied. "We'll just spend the night out here in the city square." But Lot insisted, so at last they went home with*

Demonic Genetic Mutation

him. Lot prepared a feast for them, complete with fresh bread made without yeast, and they ate. But before they retired for the night, all the men of Sodom, young and old, came from all over the city and surrounded the house. They shouted to Lot, "Where are the men who came to spend the night with you? Bring them out to us so we can have sex with them!" So Lot stepped outside to talk to them, shutting the door behind him. "Please, my brothers," he begged, "don't do such a wicked thing. Look, I have two virgin daughters. Let me bring them out to you, and you can do with them as you wish. But please, leave these men alone, for they are my guests and are under my protection."

Genesis 19:1-8

Before God destroyed Sodom and Gomorrah the Bible says that he sent two of his holy Angels to investigate the level of wickedness in the City. When Lot saw these two men, and realized that they were strangers, he invited them to spend the night in his home. Lot had no idea that these two men were actually holy Angels sent by God to the city of Sodom, to rescue Lot and his family in response to Abraham's intercession. But when the men of Sodom discovered the presence of these two men who were in Lot's custody, they started pounding on Lot's front door. They demanded that "Lot" release the two men in his house into their care, so they could have sex with them. What is interesting is that "Lot" called their sexual desire and sexual preference "wicked." We know that it is their desire to have sex with other men that "Lot" was calling wickedness, because he offered them an alternative and natural appeasement for their sexual desire. Lot offered these men his two virgin daughters in the place of his male visitors, but they refused. If these men's sexual desire for other men was genetically normal; why would Lot call their expressed desire "wickedness?"

"Do not practice homosexuality, having sex with another man as with a woman. It is a detestable sin. "A man must not defile himself by having sex with an animal. And a woman must not offer herself to a male animal to have intercourse with it. This is a perverse act.

Leviticus 18:21-23

Moses, the writer of the book of Leviticus, does not contradict "Lot's" conclusion that having sex with another man, as with a woman, is wickedness. This stern warning of God, in Leviticus 18:21, is followed immediately by another stern warning stating that a man was not to defile himself by having sex with an animal. Likewise, a woman was not to do the same, by having sexual intercourse with a male animal. Both of these acts are labeled as acts of perversion. Leviticus 18:21 flies in the face of every scientific data that may have us believe that the cultural and social phenomenon of same-sex attraction is normal, and genetically induced. Apparently, God himself doesn't think so. God is not a cruel taskmaster who can condemn anybody for simply acting out a normal sexual attraction, to members of the same sex, if such a desire was actually placed in the person's genetic makeup by God himself. Such an act would be like God judging a black man for being black, or dark skinned.

> *They traded the truth about God for a lie. So they worshiped and served the things God created instead of the Creator himself, who is worthy of eternal praise! Amen. That is why God abandoned them to their shameful desires. Even the women turned against the natural way to have sex and instead indulged in sex with each other. And the men, instead of having normal sexual relations with women, burned with lust for each other. Men did shameful things with other men, and as a result of this sin, they suffered within themselves the penalty they deserved.*
>
> Romans 1:25-27

By the time we get to the New Testament, and note the Apostle Paul's view of the phenomenon of same-sex attractions and sexual unions, he does not deviate from Lot and Moses' conclusion. The Old and New Testaments concur that same-sex attraction and same-sex sexual unions are unnatural. *By harmonizing the collective consensus of the above passages of scripture, it is clear that the ancient Hebrew Scriptures treat the phenomenon of same-sex attraction as a demonic genetic mutation.*

This is not to say or imply that gays are inherently demonic or wicked. Some of the nicest people I have met are members of the gay community. But their inherent deeply rooted sexual attraction, to members of the same-sex, is based upon a demonically engineered mutation. After the failure of the Nephilim agenda, after the devastating flood, the devil was still terrified by his memory of the ancient prophecy that God spoke against him in the Garden of Eden. I truly believe that Satan devised another plan to intercept the entrance of the Messianic seed into the earth realm. I believe that after the flood, demonic powers began to manipulate man's genetic wiring, by infusing a deep sexual attraction between people of the same sex within man's genetics. This new demonic mutation was not focused on corrupting what came out of the womb of the woman, as in the Nephilim agenda. This new demonic mutation was designed to abort the consummation of the seed and the birthing of it altogether. A person does not have to be a rocket scientist to understand that no matter how long members of the same sex have sexual intercourse with each other, they will never be able to produce the second-generation (babies). In this sense, what we commonly call the gay lifestyle is a reverse strategy of the Devil's original Nephilim agenda. The only common factor, in both scenarios, is that in both cases the Devil's plan hinged on his ability to manipulate man's DNA, to his own ends. This final passage in this chapter was not written to demonize members of the gay community. Please remember that the Lord Jesus Christ loves everybody and that He died for the sins of the whole world. But, I included it to help the global Church be better equipped in administering "Genetic salvation" to homosexuals and lesbians in a spirit of love.

LIFE APPLICATION SECTION

MEMORY VERSE

This is the book of the generations of Adam. In the day that God created man, in the likeness of God made he him; Male and female created he them; and blessed them, and called their name Adam, in the day when they were created. And Adam lived an hundred and thirty years, and begat a son in his own likeness, and after his image; and called his name Seth:

Genesis 5:1-3

REFLECTIONS

What is Genetic Mutation?

_____
_____
_____
_____
_____

What is the Nephilim Agenda?

_____
_____
_____
_____
_____

JOURNAL YOUR THOUGHTS ON THIS CHAPTER

Chapter Five

UNDERSTANDING GENERATIONAL CURSES

Then God gave the people all these instructions "I am the Lord your God, who rescued you from the land of Egypt, the place of your slavery. "You must not have any other god but me.

"You must not make for yourself an idol of any kind or an image of anything in the heavens or on the earth or in the sea. You must not bow down to them or worship them, for I, the Lord your God, am a jealous God who will not tolerate your affection for any other gods. I lay the sins of the parents upon their children; the entire family is affected—even children in the third and fourth generations of those who reject me.

Exodus 20:1-5

The Bible tells us that the *"causeless curse shall never arise."* This means that if a piece of property, or person is cursed, there is usually a legitimate reason or reasons for the same. Exodus 20:1-5 contains the nomenclature of a *Generational Curse*. Before we expound on this passage, so as to help us understand generational curses and how they work, I want to define the word "Generation."

By definition, the word "Generation" is a compound word made up of two very powerful English words. These two words are "Gene" and "Ration." A "Gene"....*is the basic unit of heredity in a living organism. All living things depend on genes. Genes hold the information to build and maintain an organism's cells and pass genetic traits to offspring.* On the other hand, the word "Ration" means the following... *A portion designated to a person or group; to supply with a ration; to limit (someone) to a specific allowance of something; to portion out (especially during a shortage of supply); to limit access to; to restrict (an activity etc)*. We also have to define the word "Curse." A "Curse"... *is something causing misery or death; a hex: an evil spell; an appeal to some supernatural power to inflict evil on someone or some group.*

We can now properly and intelligently define the spiritual phenomenon known as *"Generational Curses."* Based upon the above conjunctions we can come up with the following probable definitions of a *"Generational curse."*

A *Generational Curse* is an evil spell that is attached to a person's ration of genes.

A *Generational Curse* is an appeal to some supernatural power to inflict evil on a person or a group (family line) based upon their ration of genes.

A *Generational Curse* is a curse that is attached to a person's ration of genes.

A *Generational Curse* is something that causes misery or death that is attached to a person's ration of genes.

A *Generational Curse* is a demonic phenomenon that transports demons and demonic tendencies to the second generation, through the ration of genes that the second generation received from the first generation.

Looking at the above definitions of the phenomenon known as *Generational Curses,* it is easy to see why the devil and demonic powers love to do their dirty work through the genetics of the human race. The enemy knows that if he attaches himself to the *ration of genes* that we're passing on to our children, he will be able to multiply his diabolical influence with our children and their children's children. By far, my favorite definition of a *Generational Curse* is one that the Holy Spirit recently gave to me. I have stated it below for your benefit.

A *Generational Curse* is a demonic lien against our ration of genes, because of an unpaid spiritual bill or offence in our bloodline that the enemy feels legally justified to enforce, up to the third and fourth generation.

Unpaid Property Taxes

Let me give you an allegorical story, to help illustrate the prophetic and practical implications of the above definition, for a *Generational Curse.* A woman who lives in New York, by the name of Susie, receives a phone call that both of her wealthy parents died in a plane crash. The attorneys of Susie's deceased parents call, and instruct her to come to their law offices after the funeral, for the reading of her parent's last will and testament. When she gets to the law offices, the lawyers unseal the sealed will and testament and begin to read it. Susie discovers, to her great dismay, that her parents left her their magnificent $7 million beach house in Florida. Susie can hardly believe her ears.

Susie quickly sells her tiny apartment in New York City and moves to Florida, to take up residency in her magnificent seven million-dollar beach house. A month after living in the house that her parents left her, she gets some unexpected visitors. Lo and behold, these visitors are from the Internal Revenue Service, commonly known as the IRS. With shaky and sweaty hands, Susie welcomes the taxmen into her new house. Without mincing any words, the taxmen get to the heart of their visit.

"Susie, our records show that you are now the owner of this mansion, is this true? Yes Sir!" Susie quickly replies. *"Are you aware that there is a 2.5 million-dollar tax lien against this property for unpaid property taxes from the past five years? No Sir, I had no idea."* Susie replies. *"Since you are now the new owner of this mansion you are now responsible for paying this overdue tax lien. Failure to do so will result in this house being auctioned off by the IRS to recoup our taxes. Do you understand this? Yes Sir!"* Comes Susie's timid reply.

The above analogy does give us a graphic picture of how generational curses work. Even though Susie was not responsible for not paying the property taxes over the past five years; she nevertheless became responsible for them the moment she inherited her family's estate. *Since all general generational curses are based upon inheritance law, the above story exemplifies for us how the devil places demonic liens against our bloodline or ancestral line.* Unless this demonic lien against our lineage or genealogy is supernaturally removed, we will continue to pay a heavy price in our present for the sins of the forefathers.

The Mountain of Law

Thou shalt not bow down thyself to them, nor serve them: for I the LORD thy God am a jealous God, visiting the iniquity of the fathers upon the children unto the third and fourth generation of them that hate me;

Exodus 20:5 KJV

Perhaps the most important factor to understand about generational curses is that they are based upon the Mountain of Law. The Expression in the above verse "visiting the iniquity of the fathers upon the children" is a very interesting phrase. The word "iniquity" in the phrase refers to acts of lawlessness. *So an iniquity is a lawless act or an act against God's law.* Since God's law governs everything in creation and is the supreme law; an "iniquity" has far-reaching spiritual implications. Based upon the above passage, it is very clear that it is these iniquities that are committed by our forefathers against God's Law that opens the door for generational curses to ensue upon the following generations.

This means that all *Generational Curses* are based upon violations against God's Law. Since *Generational Curses* are byproducts of violations against God's law, it is impossible to completely overthrow *Generational Curses* without addressing the legal issues involved. This is why I believe that *Generational Curses* can never be fully overturned by those who fail to honor and satisfy God's Law in how these *Generational Curses* are settled.

The Dynamics of Law

The sting of death is sin; and the strength of sin is the law.

1 Corinthians 15:56

Since *Generational Curses* are based upon the Mountain of Law, it behooves us to understand the dynamics of Law. For as long as I can remember, I have had a deep interest in the subject of *Law and Order*. My favorite TV show is called "Law and Order." In 1 Corinthians 15:56 Paul the apostle shows us one of the most important aspects of the Law of God. The Apostle Paul tells us that the sting of death is sin; and the strength of sin is the law. This is a very powerful principle of Law. Sin does not really exist where there is no law. *In other words, there are no crimes without the Law. It is the Law that gives definition and context to crime.*

In the United States of America civilians found in possession of an assault rifle are charged with a crime. Let us suppose that there was no law on the books in American society that prohibited civilians from owning an assault rifle. Would a civilian found in possession of the same be accused of a crime? The answer is an emphatic no. This is the principle that the apostle Paul wants to teach us concerning the dynamics of Law.

Consequently, *Generational Curses* would not even be worth the paper that they are written on if there was no "Law" that demanded restitution for the iniquity of the forefathers. This is why those who try to settle and overturn

Generational Curses using prayer alone, without satisfying the demands of the Law, will experience dismal success in their efforts. This is because the "Law" is the strength of "Sin." This does not mean that the law is sinful. But, without it, sin would have no power or context.

> *For as many as are of the works of the law are under the curse: for it is written, Cursed is every one that continueth not in all things which are written in the book of the law to do them.*
>
> Galatians 3:10

In Galatians 3:10 the apostle Paul gives us another principle of Law. This principle can be summed up in this expression, *"he who is guilty of breaking one Law has broken the whole Law."* This passage also shows us that the person found guilty of breaking one element of the law of God was guilty of breaking the whole Law, and came under a curse. This principle means that the Law can only be satisfied by itself. Let me illustrate this point in an allegorical story.

1000 Traffic Tickets

Let us suppose for a moment that the police department in your city, because of one thousand traffic violations against you, has just issued a warrant for your arrest In order to save yourself from going to jail, you rush to the courthouse to pay off the traffic tickets. At the courthouse, you find yourself standing in front of a judge who beckons you to speak in your defense. Let us suppose that this is how you defend yourself. *"Your honor, I know that I'm guilty of having committed these 1000 traffic violations. But your Honor, I want to offer you a deal. I have in my hands thousands of dollars to pay for half of my traffic violations. Your Honor, since I am giving the court such a great sum of money, I believe that you should forgo judgment against me for the remaining 500 traffic violations."*

What do you think would be the response of any self-respecting judge who understands the dynamics of Law? I believe that the judge would tell you that his courtroom of Law is no place for such negotiations. He would also remind you that that the large sum of money you are paying for 500 of the 1000 tickets is simply what is required of you by law. It is not a favor that you are bequeathing on the courtroom. Furthermore, the judge would probably tell you that if you do not go ahead and pay for the remaining 500 traffic violations, you will be hauled off to jail.

The Dynamics of Lineage

And Joseph also went up from Galilee, out of the city of Nazareth, into Judaea, unto the city of David, which is called Bethlehem; (because he was of the house and lineage of David:)

Luke 2:4

The above allegory helps to illustrate what I call the dynamics of lineage. *Generational curses are based upon iniquities that have taken place in a particular ancestral bloodline or lineage since the first progenitor.* Since such is the case, it is important to understand the dynamics of lineage. Let us first define the word "lineage." *"Lineage" is a sequence of species that form a line of descent. Each new species is the direct result of speciation from an immediate ancestral species.*

Based upon the above definition of the word lineage, we can safely say that the length of any *Generational Curse* is based upon the lineage of the person who is affected by the same. This is because in layman's terms a lineage is simply the "age" of the ancestral line. This means that that if the lineage or the age of the ancestral line is 1000 years; repenting over the iniquities of the last 100 years, that we can remember, does not release us from the iniquities of the other 900 years. This principle is the same as a man who owes the state for 1000 traffic violations but only manages to pay for 500. The Law will still consider him responsible for the remaining 500 unpaid traffic violations.

This would explain why the traditional way of breaking *Generational Curses* has not been eminently successful. The people who seek deliverance from *Generational Curses*, from deliverance ministers who do not understand the spiritual technology contained in this book, end up having to come back again and again in search of more prayers. This book *"Breaking Generational Curses under the Order of Melchizedek"* is designed to show you how God can supernaturally take you out of your natural lineage, by the supernatural superimposition of His divinity upon your humanity.

LIFE APPLICATION SECTION

MEMORY VERSE

Then God gave the people all these instructions "I am the Lord your God, who rescued you from the land of Egypt, the place of your slavery. "You must not have any other god but me.

"You must not make for yourself an idol of any kind or an image of anything in the heavens or on the earth or in the sea. You must not bow down to them or worship them, for I, the Lord your God, am a jealous God who will not tolerate your affection for any other gods. I lay the sins of the parents upon their children; the entire family is affected—even children in the third and fourth generations of those who reject me.

Exodus 20:1-5

REFLECTIONS

What is a Generational Curse?

___

___

___

___

___

What is a Genetic Anomaly?

___

___

___

___

___

JOURNAL YOUR THOUGHTS ON THIS CHAPTER

CHAPTER Six

THE ANATOMY OF A GENERATIONAL CURSE

Then God gave the people all these instructions "I am the Lord your God, who rescued you from the land of Egypt, the place of your slavery. "You must not have any other god but me.

"You must not make for yourself an idol of any kind or an image of anything in the heavens or on the earth or in the sea. You must not bow down to them or worship them, for I, the Lord your God, am a jealous God who will not tolerate your affection for any other gods. I lay the sins of the parents upon their children; the entire family is affected—even children in the third and fourth generations of those who reject me.

Exodus 20:1-5

In this chapter our investigation into the nomenclature of the spiritual technology of overturning generational curses and healing genetic anomalies demands that we analyze the " anatomy off a generational curse." To help us dive into the depths of this analysis we must clearly defined the science of anatomy.

The online thesaurus dictionary defines the science of anatomy as follows:

The bodily structure of the plant or an animal or any of its parts.

The science of the shape and structure of organisms and their parts.

The treatise on anatomic science.

Dissection of a plant or animal to study the structure, position and the interrelation of its various parts.

A skeleton.

The human body.

A detailed examination or analysis.

Essentially the science of anatomy deals with understanding the internal matrix of any living organism. This science examines the different parts or organs of any living organism and how these individual parts interrelate within the structure of the living organism. Consequently the science of spiritual anatomy, which is a higher and more credible science than the science of natural anatomy, also involves the surgical and spiritual analysis of the internal matrix of any spiritual organism or technology. In our endeavor to understand generational curses and how we can break them permanently, it would be prudent of us to, understand the spiritual anatomy of a "generational curse."

In my opinion there are very few scriptural passages that capture the complete anatomy of a generational curse like Exodus 20:1-5. This is why I will use this passage to bring you into a deep understanding of the spiritual anatomy of a generational curse.

God

Then God gave the people all these instructions "I am the Lord your God, who rescued you from the land of Egypt, the place of your slavery. "You must not have any other god but me.

Exodus 20:1-3

The first and most important element in the anatomy of a "Generational Curse" is "God." This might surprise a lot of believers that I would include God in the anatomy of a Generational Curse. The context in which I include "God" in the anatomy of a generational curse is to simply establish the fact that the Bible teaches that "Sin" is primarily against God before it is against anything else. After David committed adultery with Uriah's wife he cried in deep repentance to God and this is what he says in the fifty-first Psalm... *"Against You (God) and only You have I sinned!"* This is a very surprising statement coming from David considering that he sinned with another man's wife. I would have thought that the first verse in the fifty-first Psalm should have read as follows... *"Against You (God) and Uriah have I sinned."* But apparently King David understood that "Sin" in its very essence is always against God because we all live in God's world.

This is why before I pray for people to be delivered from generational curses and genetic anomalies; I first lead them in a prayer of repentance to God. This is because I realize that the sin that opened the door to the entrance of the generational curse is first and foremost an action against God's holiness. By leading them through a prayer of repentance before asking God to deliver them guarantees God's favor and power over their situation.

God's Law

Know ye not, brethren, (for I speak to them that know the law,) how that the law hath dominion over a man as long as he liveth?

Romans 7:1 KJV

The second element of the anatomy of a generational curse is "God's law." We have already mentioned the fact that the strength of sin is the law. This means that where there is no Law, sin is powerless. This is what the apostle Paul means in the book of Romans when he says that " before the giving of the Law, sin was in the world but it was not imputed." Without the "Concept of Law" in any society it is impossible to clearly define "crime and punishment." Since all Generational curses deal with both crime and punishment, they can only exist to the extent that they represent the consequences of violating God's law.

This is why I focus on addressing the legalities behind any Generational curse before proceeding to pray against them. It is impossible to completely eliminate the claims of any Generational curse on any person's life without healing the "breach" against God's law that transpired in their past.

An Iniquity

"You must not make for yourself an idol of any kind or an image of anything in the heavens or on the earth or in the sea. 5 You must not bow down to them or worship them, for I, the Lord your God, am a jealous God who will not tolerate your affection for any other gods. I lay the sins of the parents upon their children; the entire family is affected—even children in the third and fourth generations of those who reject me.

Exodus 20:1-5

The third element of the anatomy of a Generational curse is called "iniquity." An iniquity is a "lawless act against God's law." Based upon the above passage it is clear that the Lord went to great length to list down actions that He considered gross violations of His holiness or supreme law. This means that every action that violates God's law that is perpetuated by members of any bloodline creates an "iniquity" against that particular bloodline.

Since iniquities are actions against God's law in any bloodline, the longer that a person's lineage is the greater the number of iniquities against that particular bloodline. This is why the traditional method of breaking generation curses by rehearsing and repenting of the past iniquities that we can remember does not work well; because most of us do not know the number of iniquities attached to our bloodline from many years ago. This book suggests a more excellent way of overturning governing iniquities in our bloodline.

A Traceable Lineage (Bloodline)

You must not bow down to them or worship them, for I, the Lord your God, am a jealous God who will not tolerate your affection for any other gods. I lay the sins of the parents upon their children; the entire family is affected—even children in the third and fourth generations of those who reject me.

Exodus 20:5

The fourth element in the anatomy of a "Generational curse" is a "Traceable Lineage of Bloodline." No generational curse can operate were there is no traceable lineage or genealogy. You cannot effect or impose a generational curse in the absence of a traceable lineage or bloodline. This is why the High Priest over the Order of Melchizedek is so powerful because He has no traceable earthly genealogy or end of life.

Since all generational curses are based upon "curses" attached to the "ration of genes" that a person received from his or her ancestors; tracing the bloodline that the "ration of genes" belong to is extremely important. When homicide detectives come upon a scene of a crime they quickly set up parameters to secure the crime scene. After doing so, they start looking for fingerprints. Once they find fingerprints these fingerprints are swabbed for DNA. The DNA samples collected from the crime scene are then sent to the FBI lab where it is analyzed against the vast FBI database.

When the DNA sample taken from the crime scene matches that of a person on the FBI's database the police know immediately that they have a "suspect and possible murderer."

Generational curses operate on the same principle. The homicide detectives in our above story represent "demonic enforcers" who are responsible for enforcing the penalties that are attached to the iniquities that are attached to the genealogy under investigation.

Demonic Enforcers

He that diggeth a pit shall fall into it; and whoso breaketh an hedge, a serpent shall bite him.
Ecclesiastes 10:8 (King James Version)

Shouldest not thou also have had compassion on thy fellow servant, even as I had pity on thee? And his lord was wroth, and delivered him to the tormentors, till he should pay all that was due unto him. So likewise shall my heavenly Father do also unto you, if ye from your hearts forgive not every one his brother their trespasses.
Matthew 18:33-35 (King James Version)

The fifth and final element in the anatomy of a generational curse are "Demonic Enforcers." The writer of Ecclesiastes 10:8 tells us that whosoever breaks a hedge will be beaten by a snake. In the bible "snakes" more often than not represent "demonic spirits" that bite the inhabitants of the earth with their poison. The Lord Jesus Christ called these diabolical spirits "tormentors or enforcers." Jesus Christ made it clear that demons have legal grounds to oppress people who do not walk in forgiveness towards other people.

These demonic enforcers are the ones who keep score against every lineage or bloodline on earth that is guilty of violating God's law and holiness. It is interesting to note that the same devil that tempts the world to rebel against God's law is also the same one who punishes people for doing so. The spiritual technology for breaking generational curses that is contained in this book is able to annihilate the diabolical assignments of these demonic enforcers.

LIFE APPLICATION SECTION

MEMORY VERSE

Shouldest not thou also have had compassion on thy fellow servant, even as I had pity on thee? And his lord was wroth, and delivered him to the tormentors, till he should pay all that was due unto him. So likewise shall my heavenly Father do also unto you, if ye from your hearts forgive not every one his brother their trespasses.

Matthew 18:33-35 (King James Version)

REFLECTIONS

What is Spiritual Anatomy?

_____
_____
_____
_____
_____

Name one of the elements of the Anatomy of a Generational Curse

_____
_____
_____
_____
_____

JOURNAL YOUR THOUGHTS ON THIS CHAPTER

CHAPTER
Seven

THE LAW OF INHERITANCE

Then God gave the people all these instructions "I am the Lord your God, who rescued you from the land of Egypt, the place of your slavery. "You must not have any other god but me.

"You must not make for yourself an idol of any kind or an image of anything in the heavens or on the earth or in the sea. You must not bow down to them or worship them, for I, the Lord your God, am a jealous God who will not tolerate your affection for any other gods. I lay the sins of the parents upon their children; the entire family is affected—even children in the third and fourth generations of those who reject me.

Exodus 20:1-5

In this chapter we will examine the law that governs *"Generational Curses"* and *"Generational Blessings."* This law is called inheritance law. Inheritance law is the only law in the spirit world and in the natural that controls the passage of property or genetics from one family member to another. We can also say that inheritance law controls the rights of passage. Inheritance law truly comes in handy when you're dealing with how to pass on the property of a deceased relative. Probate courts deal with inheritance issues all day long. Another institution on earth that is the best example of the power of Inheritance law is the institution of marriage. We will examine the dynamics of inheritance law with the institution of marriage later on. But since this book is about breaking generational curses and genetic anomalies we will first look at the dynamics of inheritance law within the field of genetics.

Inheritance Law in the Genetics

Mendelian inheritance (or Mendelian genetics or Mendelism) is a set of primary tenets relating to the transmission of hereditary characteristics from parent organisms to their offspring; it underlies much of genetics. They were initially derived from the work of Gregor Mendel published in 1865 and 1866, which was "re-discovered" in 1900, and were initially very controversial. When they were integrated with the chromosome theory of inheritance by Thomas Hunt Morgan in 1915, they became the core of classical genetics.

Heredity is the passing of traits to offspring (from its parent or ancestors). This is the process by which an offspring cell or organism acquires or becomes predisposed to the characteristics of its parent cell or organism. (From Free Encyclopedia)

The work of Gregor Mendel and Thomas Hunt Morgan in the field of genetics is unrivaled. It is because of the work of these two brilliant genetic scientists that has helped us to know for certain that "Genes" are responsible for much of the transmission of hereditary characteristics from parent organisms to their offspring. It is clear then that inheritance law governs the transfer of genes from one generation to the next.

Inheritance Law

Since we have arrived at the conclusion that the transmission of hereditary characteristics from parent organisms to their offspring is based upon the "ration of genes" that are transmitted from one generation to another; we cannot overturn generational curses and genetic anomalies without breaking the power of the inheritance law that governs the same. Since generational curses are based upon iniquities that are attached to the *"ration" of "genes"* that a person inherited from their natural bloodline; we have to find a way to legally release people from their compromised *"ration" of "genes."*

A while back I became a naturalized American citizen. I had gone through a long legal process of becoming an American citizen. Even though I was born in Africa, I knew that I could change my inheritance if I went through the legal channels of becoming an American citizen. When the Department of Homeland Security and Immigration Services informed me that my application for citizenship had been approved I was overjoyed. I was asked to come to the immigration center to say my oath of allegiance so I could become a citizen. After I said the oath of allegiance an official of the United States government declared me a US citizen. As soon as they pronounced me an American citizen they told me that I now had all the rights and privileges of an American citizen just like Americans who were born in the United States. By becoming an American citizen I had legally excused myself from being a citizen of Zambia the country of my birth.

The purpose of sharing my story is to demonstrate that they are legal channels and procedures in the spirit world and the natural world by which we can change our inheritance. Applying this principle we can begin to see how God can use the same dynamics of inheritance law to cut off any and all generational curses that have been attached to us because of our natural bloodlines if we have legally denounced our allegiance to them in order to embrace our citizenship in God's Kingdom.

Marriage and Inheritance Law

This explains why a man leaves his father and mother and is joined to his wife, and the two are united into one.

Genesis 2:24

At the beginning of this chapter I made mention of the fact that the institution of marriage is the best vehicle for expressing the power and the inner workings of the law of inheritance. Marriage can change a person's social and economic status in a single day. I am going to tell you an allegorical story just to demonstrate the dynamics of inheritance law and how it provides us with the perfect solution for absolution from *"Generational Curses and Genetic anomalies."*

An Allegory

Suzy Piere is a beautiful woman who leaves in the South of France. She is smart and funny but has lived a very disadvantaged life. She was born in a family of peasants. Her family is one of the poorest families in the South of France. Her family's poverty was so severe that Suzy was forced to leave school and work as a maid at a very expensive and famous resort. Meanwhile in the United States of America a man by the name of John Adams who lives in Hollywood California was getting ready to board a private jet bound for the South of France to stay at the same resort where Suzy works. Forbes business news listed Mr. John Adam's net worth at 1.5 billion dollars.

One uneventful day Suzy went to work as usual. And when she got to the hotel to start her normal duties her manager called her aside and told her that she was being given a very special assignment that morning. She was to clean the penthouse of a very wealthy man by the name of John Adams from the United States of America. Suzy then headed to the penthouse to clean it knowing that if she did a good job she would score great points with her manager.

When she got to the penthouse occupied by Mr. John Adams, she paused and then tapped the front door gently. A commanding voice from within said, "Please come in." She quickly entered and once inside she busied herself with her cleaning duties. Unbeknown to her, her beauty had left Mr. John Adams breathless. In his eyes she was more beautiful than an angel. If there was such a thing as love at first sight he knew that he had been smitten. To cut a long story short Mr. John Adams ends up marrying Suzy Piere and brings her to America. She arrives at their private airstrip in Hollywood as Mrs. Suzy Adams.

So here comes the million-dollar question, "After her marriage to Mr. John Adams is Suzy Piere still poverty stricken or is she a billionaire?" Anybody who understands how inheritance law works in marriage knows that when she married Mr. Adams everything he owned became her property. Even the change in name from Suzy Piere to Suzy Adams was a guarantee that her fortunes had changed dramatically.

What About our Marriage to Christ?

As the Scriptures say, "A man leaves his father and mother and is joined to his wife, and the two are united into one." This is a great mystery, but it is an illustration of the way Christ and the church are one. So again I say, each man must love his wife as he loves himself, and the wife must respect her husband.

Ephesians 5:31-33

If the above allegorical story has any truth to it concerning the dynamics of inheritance law within the institution of marriage; then we have unraveled the mystery to breaking Generational curses permanently. Instead of trying to fix our old sin compromised and broken down lineage we must allow our marriage to Christ to alter our inheritance. Our marriage to Christ then affords us the legal grounds for demanding our complete absolution from all the generational penalties attached to our natural lineages.

The Law of Inheritance

The bible is clear that Jesus Christ was the perfect symmetry of humanity and divinity. In His divinity "Christ" has "no earthly genealogy" that can hold him to the past and in His humanity He represents total genetic perfection. In His humanity He had a bloodline that was a reservoir of genetically and spiritually flawless DNA. In marrying Him we inherit both His lack of a traceable human genealogy that "Generational Curses" can be attached to and also His enduring righteousness. In marrying Him we also inherit His genetically and spiritually perfect DNA; which in turn becomes superimposed over our broken down genetics. The superimposition of His divinity on our humanity provides us with the release from *"Generational curses"* that we so desire. The superimposition of His perfect humanity over our broken down humanity provides us with an antidote that we need to heal every genetic anomaly in our life.

LIFE APPLICATION SECTION

MEMORY VERSE

To illustrate the point further, Jesus told them this story: "A man had two sons. The younger son told his father, 'I want my share of your estate now before you die.' So his father agreed to divide his wealth between his sons.

Luke 15:11-12

REFLECTIONS

What is Inheritance Law?

_____
_____
_____
_____
_____

How does our Marriage to Christ help us break free of all Generational Curses?

_____
_____
_____
_____
_____

JOURNAL YOUR THOUGHTS ON THIS CHAPTER

Chapter
Eight

SUPERNATURAL GENETIC ENGINEERING

We have finally come to one of my favorite chapters in this book. This chapter, above all chapters, will focus on the whole process of supernatural genetic engineering. This chapter will clearly show us that God is able to heal, restore and reconfigure mankind's broken down genetics. This chapter will show us that God is able to overturn and repair any form of demonic genetic mutation inside the human genome. This chapter will show us that before genetic scientists and forensic pathologists discovered the phenomenon known as Genetic engineering, God revealed this technology to Jacob.

For all practical purposes, Jacob became one of the richest men in Syria when he was working for his uncle Laban. This is because God showed him how to manipulate the genetics of the surrounding animals for his own posterity. Before going deeper into this writing, I want us to first define the term genetic engineering.

Definition: *"Genetic engineering" is the alteration of genetic code by artificial means, and is therefore different from traditional selective breeding.*

"What wages do you want?" Laban asked again. Jacob replied, "Don't give me anything. Just do this one thing, and I'll continue to tend and watch over your flocks. Let me inspect your flocks today and remove all the sheep and goats that are speckled or spotted, along with all the black sheep. Give these to me as my wages. In the future, when you check on the animals you have given me as my wages, you'll see that I have been honest. If you find in my flock any goats without speckles or spots, or any sheep

that are not black, you will know that I have stolen them from you." "All right," Laban replied. "It will be as you say." But that very day Laban went out and removed the male goats that were streaked and spotted, all the female goats that were speckled and spotted or had white patches, and all the black sheep. He placed them in the care of his own sons, who took them a three days' journey from where Jacob was. Meanwhile, Jacob stayed and cared for the rest of Laban's flock. Then Jacob took some fresh branches from poplar, almond, and plane trees and peeled off strips of bark, making white streaks on them. Then he placed these peeled branches in the watering troughs where the flocks came to drink, for that was where they mated. And when they mated in front of the white-streaked branches, they gave birth to young that were streaked, speckled, and spotted. Jacob separated those lambs from Laban's flock. And at mating time he turned the flock to face Laban's animals that were streaked or black. This is how he built his own flock instead of increasing Laban's. Whenever the stronger females were ready to mate, Jacob would place the peeled branches in the watering troughs in front of them. Then they would mate in front of the branches. But he didn't do this with the weaker ones, so the weaker lambs belonged to Laban, and the stronger ones were Jacob's. As a result, Jacob became very wealthy, with large flocks of sheep and goats, male and female servants, and many camels and donkeys.

Genesis 30:37-43

After twenty years of working for his uncle and father-in-law by the name of Laban; Jacob saw that he was still living in abject poverty, even though his anointing and skill at attending animals was releasing an abundance of material blessings in Laban's house. Depressed and disturbed by his personal lack of financial achievement, Jacob asked his father-in-law to let him go back to his father's country. But, Laban was not willing to let go of his most productive employee. So, he began to plead with Jacob to stay.

Jacob's father-in-law told him that all he had to do was name his price and he would have it, provided he continued to work for Laban. In this atmosphere of negotiation, Jacob made a very unusual request to Laban. It was a request that any scientific mind would have judged foolish and ill advised. Jacob made a suggestion that at the time was considered to be genetically impossible. Jacob told his father-in-law that he would work for him a couple more years, on the condition that he allowed Jacob to take as his wages spotted animals that came out as offspring of one-colored animals.

Laban could hardly believe what he was hearing. He was now convinced that his son-in-law was probably more foolish than he had thought. He was sure that Jacob was going to be working for him for the rest of his life. Jacob told Laban that that he wanted him to take every animal among his livestock that was spotted in any form or fashion, and remove them far away from Jacob. This meant that Jacob would only be taking care of animals that had one full color. Jacob then dropped the genetic bombshell, when he told his father-in-law that it would come to pass that any one-colored animal, that produced sported offspring, would belong to Jacob.

After Jacob made this unusual request, Laban was excited beyond belief. He had no idea that the God of Abraham and Isaac had given him a revolutionary scientific business idea. It was an idea that was thousands of years ahead of its time concerning the field of genetic science. What Jacob was suggesting had no prior precedence in both nature and science. What Jacob was suggesting was tantamount to asking a black couple to give birth to a white baby. In Laban's mind, and the intellectuals of his day, Jacob's decision doomed him to a life of poverty and servitude. Laban was no scientist, but he knew that what Jacob was suggesting was impossible.

Destiny Altering Prophetic Dreams

"One time during the mating season, I had a dream and saw that the male goats mating with the females were streaked, speckled, and spotted. Then in my dream, the angel of God said to me, 'Jacob!' And I replied, 'Yes, here I am.' *"The angel said, 'Look up, and you will see that only the streaked, speckled, and spotted males are mating with the females of your flock. For I have seen how Laban has treated you. I am the God who appeared to you at Bethel, the place where you anointed the pillar of stone and made your vow to me. Now get ready and leave this country and return to the land of your birth.'"*

Genesis 31:10-13

While Laban was rejoicing about what he thought was Jacobs' ill devised decision; Jacob was telling his wives how God had given him the idea of opening the oldest genetic engineering firm in the world. Jacob told his wives about the destiny altering prophetic dream that God had given him. In the dream, he saw God give him an abundance of spotted livestock from animals that are one color.

After his new employment contract with his employer Laban had been signed, Jacob unveiled the rest of the divine business plan and methodology. The Bible says that Jacob went and cut fresh branches from a tree, then took a knife, and cut white spots on all the branches. Jacob crisscrossed these branches that he had created. And, it came to pass that whenever anyone of the strong one colored livestock began mating; Jacob placed the photo of the crisscrossed branches in front of them. Brain scientists know that in highly emotional situations, the reticular formation part of the brain opens up. And, any image that goes into the brain during such moments has a brain and genetic altering effect.

To everyone's amazement, the one-colored sheep and one-colored oxen all began to produce offspring that were all spotted. This process continued until Jacob had more sheep and cattle.

The Technology of Names

When the baby was eight days old, they all came for the circumcision ceremony. They wanted to name him Zechariah, after his father. But Elizabeth said, "No! His name is John!" "What?" they exclaimed. "There is no one in all your family by that name." So they used gestures to ask the baby's father what he wanted to name him. He motioned for a writing tablet, and to everyone's surprise he wrote, "His name is John."

Luke 1:59-63

And he said, Thy name shall be called no more Jacob, but Israel: for as a prince hast thou power with God and with men, and hast prevailed.

Genesis 32:28 KJV

These two Scripture passages strongly suggest that names play a critical role in determining the nature of a thing and how it ultimately functions. Before Isaac was born God called out his name. Before King Josiah was born, God called out his name and announced his destiny as a reformer. Before the birth of the prophet John the Baptist, the angel Gabriel appeared to his father Zachariah and gave him explicit instructions, to name his firstborn son John.

The angel Gabriel appears one final time, in the New Testament, to announce the birth of the world's promised Messiah—Jesus. When the angel Gabriel appeared to Joseph in a dream, he told him to call the child who was going to be born out of Mary's womb Jesus! Jesus means "Savior." These incidences clearly showcase the importance of names in the spirit realm. An incorrect name can give birth to an inaccurate expression of a person, or an entity's intended purpose.

Supernatural Genetic Reconfiguration

And out of the ground the LORD God formed every beast of the field, and every fowl of the air; and brought them unto Adam to see what he would call them: and whatsoever Adam called every living creature, that was the name thereof.

Genesis 2:19 KJV

I am afraid that many members of the Body of Christ do not really respect the "technology of names" as much as God does. But, the truth is, this ancient spiritual technology is the method that God uses to determine the capacity, function, and nature of a thing. God imparted this technology of names to Adam. The Bible says that God brought all the animals on earth to Adam, to see what he would call or name them. The Bible tells us that whatever name Adam gave to any animal; the name would enshrine that particular animal's purpose, potential and nature.

I truly believe that the technology of names is one of the primary spiritual technologies that God uses, to supernaturally engineer or reconfigure the broken down genetics, of the sons and daughters of men. In my case, for instance, several years ago God changed my last name from "Mbepa" to "Myles". Immediately after this supernatural name change, I began to experience quantum leaps in the growth of my ministry. It suffices to say that some people who want to break free of "Generational Curses" may need a total name change in the natural; but God uses different strokes for different folks.

# LIFE APPLICATION SECTION

MEMORY VERSE

And out of the ground the LORD God formed every beast of the field, and every fowl of the air; and brought them unto Adam to see what he would call them: and whatsoever Adam called every living creature, that was the name thereof.

Genesis 2:19 KJV

REFLECTIONS

What is Genetic Engineering?

_____
_____
_____
_____

What is the Technology of Names?

_____
_____
_____
_____

JOURNAL YOUR THOUGHTS ON THIS CHAPTER

Chapter Nine

THE ORDER OF MELCHIZEDEK

After Abram returned from his victory over Kedorlaomer and all his allies, the king of Sodom went out to meet him in the valley of Shaveh (that is, the King's Valley). And Melchizedek, the king of Salem and a priest of God Most High, brought Abram some bread and wine. Melchizedek blessed Abram with this blessing: "Blessed be Abram by God Most High, Creator of heaven and earth. And blessed be God Most High, who has defeated your enemies for you." Then Abram gave Melchizedek a tenth of all the goods he had recovered.

Genesis 14:17-20

Defining the Order of Melchizedek:

In the passage of scripture from the book of Isaiah 51:1-2, we are commanded by the Bible to look to Abraham. Why would God command us to look to Abraham? This is because God set a prophetic pattern for us to follow in Abraham. Since we are the seed of Abraham, everything that affects Abraham affects us today. Moses, the writer of the book of Genesis, tells us of the prophetic encounter that Abraham had with this eternal king-priest, who came from the heavenly kingdom. This high priest was known as Melchizedek and he presided over an eternal order. The apostle Paul, the writer of the book of Hebrews, has a lot to say about the order of Melchizedek. To get an in-depth analysis of the spiritual ramifications of this eternal order, please read my book <u>The Order of Melchizedek</u>.

Under this chapter I will do my best to give you the prophetic overview of the nature, and the inner workings, of this eternal order. I will first begin by defining the *Order of Melchizedek*. What is the Order of Melchizedek? I am glad that you asked me. There are three definitions of the Order of Melchizedek. I will quickly list these three definitions as the Holy Spirit gave them to me:

The Order of Melchizedek is the eternal royal priesthood of Jesus Christ before He came to our planet through the virgin birth.

The Order of Melchizedek is Jesus Christ putting on flesh and walking among us.

The Order of Melchizedek is an eternal royal spiritual order of Kings and priests. These kings and priests have both covenantal and custodial rights to advance and teach the gospel of the Kingdom, until the kingdoms of this world have become the Kingdom of God, and of His Christ.

We can see clearly from the above definitions that this eternal order, that intercepted Abraham in the Valley of the Kings in the book of Genesis, was no ordinary earthly agency. The high priest over this eternal order was also no ordinary man. If we confess that we are the seed of Abraham, and that Christ died so that the blessing of Abraham might come upon the Gentiles, then we have to rediscover the present day implications of the Order of Melchizedek. By observing these definitions, it is clear that every born-again and God-fearing child of God is a member of the order of Melchizedek.

But I want to go deeper into the definition of The *Order of Melchizedek*, by breaking down the phrase *"The Order of Melchizedek."* As you can see, this phrase is made up of two very powerful words. One is a word taken from the English language, the other is a word born out of the ancient Hebrew language. The first part of this phrase is the word *"Order."* What is order? According to the Webster dictionary "Order" is defined as follows; "*Order* is a condition in which each thing is properly disposed with reference to other things and to its purpose; in a methodical or harmonious arrangement." The word order is also defined as "conformity or obedience to Law, or an established authority."

My co-Host for our TV talk show *"the Kingdom in the marketplace"* (on one of our broadcasts), asked me a very important question that really needs to be answered. He asked me, "Dr. Myles why is the order of Melchizedek an order?" This was my response; I told him that the order of Melchizedek is an order because God always sets a governing order around anything that He has ever created. This principle sets the premise for the Law of Divine Order. The above definitions are very revealing, they unmask why the Order of Melchizedek is an eternal order, before it is anything else. It is an eternal order, which governs everything that God created in nature, including fallen Angels and man's DNA. This is why the devil and his coalition of demons are so terrified of the global church rediscovering the Order of Melchizedek.

Now let us dissect the second Hebrew word in the phrase *"The Order of Melchizedek."* The word "Melchizedek" is an ancient Hebrew compound word that consists of two powerful Aramaic words. The first word "Melech or Melek" means "King" and "Zedek or Zadok" means "righteousness" or "priest." *The Order of Melchizedek* therefore is an eternal order governed by a righteous King-priest who has complete authority over all of God's created order; So that everything in creation is properly disposed to each other with reference to God's purpose. On a genetic level, the order of Melchizedek will cause every strand of DNA to be properly disposed to each other, with reference to God's purpose for our lives.

Why We Need the Order of Melchizedek:

After Abram returned from his victory over Kedorlaomer and all his allies, the king of Sodom went out to meet him in the valley of Shaveh (that is, the King's Valley). And Melchizedek, the king of Salem and a priest of God Most High, brought Abram some bread and wine. Melchizedek blessed Abram with this blessing: "Blessed be Abram by God Most High, Creator of heaven and earth. And blessed be God Most High, who has defeated your enemies for you." Then Abram gave Melchizedek a tenth of all the goods he had recovered. The king of Sodom said to Abram "Give back my people who were captured. But you may keep for yourself all the goods you have recovered." Abram replied to the king of Sodom, "I solemnly swear to the Lord, God Most High, Creator of heaven and earth, that I will not take so much as a single thread or sandal thong from what belongs to you. Otherwise you might say, 'I am the one who made Abram rich.'

Genesis 14:17-23

In this passage, we will quickly look at why we need the order of Melchizedek in bullet point fashion:

- We need the Order of Melchizedek to introduce us to the eternal King-Priest, who is over the Kingdom that we are called to REPRESENT!

We need the Order of Melchizedek to bring us into a "Living Covenant" with God:

- Transforming our "Faith Promise" into a "Covenant Promise."
- We need the Order of Melchizedek to introduce us to the "Bread of Deliverance" and the "Wine of Revelation."
- We need the Order of Melchizedek to "Intercept" the "King of Sodom" who is attacking, compromising and destroying the Church in the Marketplace.
- We need the Order of Melchizedek to "Purify and Sanctify" the Church's "Avenues for Revenue."
- We need the Order of Melchizedek to "Shut down" the wells of Greed, that are "Compromising" Kingdom citizens in the Marketplace.
- We need the Order of Melchizedek to help Kingdom citizens (the seed of Abraham) break free of all Generational Curses and Genetic Anomalies.
- We need the Order of Melchizedek to give us the "Grace" to "Live Above" the "Perversity" in our generation.
- We need the Order of Melchizedek to introduce us (the Body of Christ) to "Real Kingdom Wealth."
- We need the Order of Melchizedek to give "Leaders" in the "Church" and the "Marketplace" a "Heart" for the Second generation.

David Discovers the Order of Melchizedek:

The Lord said to my Lord, "Sit in the place of honor at my right hand until I humble your enemies, making them a footstool under your feet." The Lord will extend your powerful kingdom from Jerusalem; you will rule over your enemies. When you go to war, your people will serve you willingly. You are arrayed in holy garments, and your strength will be renewed each day like the morning dew. The Lord has taken an oath and will not break his vow: "You are a priest forever in the order of Melchizedek."

Psalm 110:1-4

As King David continued looking for a more excellent way of approaching the presence of God, something supernatural happened. During one of his "devotions of everlasting desire," God opened a portal through the heavens and gave him access. David found himself in the heavenly realms, in the midst of a very important conversation between the Godhead. This divine conversation was between God the Father and God the Son. The revelation was going to answer David's deepest desire to get close to God's presence, without the fear of divine retribution.

In summary, this is what King David heard during the divine encounter. "The LORD said to my Lord, 'Sit at My right hand, till I make your enemies your footstool. The LORD has sworn and will not relent; you are a priest forever, according to the order of Melchizedek (Psalm 110:1, 4)." As God's flashlight of revelation flooded David's soul, the far-reaching spiritual implications of what God had shown him began to sink in.

To David's complete surprise, the divine conversation within the Godhead was centered on a heavenly priesthood. That priesthood was not functioning in its official capacity within the nation of Israel. Since the day of his birth, David had lived under the spiritual influence of the Levitical priestly Order. David also knew that since he was not born a Levite, he was excluded from the Covenant of Levi. He knew that no matter how much he loved God, he could never have the close proximity of the presence of God that he so desperately desired. He knew that under the Levitical priesthood, the penalty for touching the Ark of God for a non-Levite was instant death. This rule did not sit well with David. His only desire was to touch God in a very meaningful way.

The more David listened to the divine conversation the more excited he became. He realized that God also had a driving desire to be touched by His people, and to live among them. David realized that he had discovered the most powerful priestly Order that operates from within the realms of eternity. David could clearly see that under this priestly Order of Melchizedek Christ was the everlasting High Priest. Also, he could see that there was no veil of restriction between God and His people. David also realized that under this priestly Order, every one of God's holy children can hear the voice of God and walk in His divine power, in the beauty of holiness.

Paul's Apologetic Treatise on the Order of Melchizedek

Even though Jesus was God's Son, he learned obedience from the things he suffered. In this way, God qualified him as a perfect High Priest, and he became the source of eternal salvation for all those who obey him. And God designated him to be a

> *High Priest in the order of Melchizedek. There is much more we would like to say about this, but it is difficult to explain, especially since you are spiritually dull and don't seem to listen. You have been believers so long now that you ought to be teaching others. Instead, you need someone to teach you again the basic things about God's word. You are like babies who need milk and cannot eat solid food.*
>
> Hebrews 5:8-12

Of the post Calvary apostles of Jesus Christ, none is as important as the apostle Paul within the economy of the kingdom of God. There are three historic figures: Abraham, David and Paul, whom God used to reveal the order of Melchizedek. But, the Lord Jesus Christ gave the apostle Paul a deeper understanding of this eternal order. Writing to his fellow Hebrew brothers, the great apostle Paul wrote one of the most powerful apologetic discourses on the order of Melchizedek. Paul's primary goal for writing the book of Hebrews was to demonstrate to fellow Jewish believers the utter superiority of the Order of Melchizedek, over the Old Testament Levitical priesthood, and its on-going impact on New Testament believers.

Fortunately for us, Paul's writing to the Hebrews contains the antidote for breaking the phenomenon known as generational curses, as well as an antidote for the healing of all types of genetic anomalies. In Hebrews chapter 5, the apostle Paul rebukes some of the Hebrew believers (that he was writing to), by telling them that he had so many things to tell them about the nature and inner workings of the Order of Melchizedek, but they had become dull of hearing. The apostle Paul told some people, within his Hebrew audience, that they had become like babies needing spiritual milk, instead of the meat of God's Word. Paul's rebuke exposes why so many members of the Body of Christ are not experiencing the Order of Melchizedek in its fullest power. The Order of Melchizedek will remain a mystery to members of the Body of Christ who are addicted to living on spiritual milk, and have no desire to press into the deeper things of God. Yet, the answers to many of the Church's problems are hinged on our ability to understand the inner workings of this eternal order.

No Traceable Genealogy

> *For this Melchisedec, king of Salem, priest of the most high God, who met Abraham returning from the slaughter of the kings, and blessed him; To whom also Abraham gave a tenth part of all; first being by interpretation King of righteousness, and after*

The Order of Melchizedek

that also King of Salem, which is, King of peace; Without father, without mother, without descent, having neither beginning of days, nor end of life; but made like unto the Son of God; abideth a priest continually.

Hebrews 7:1-3 KJV

The first three verses of Hebrews chapter seven contain the nomenclature for the most potent spiritual antidote, against the cancer of generational iniquity. The first two verses focus our attention on the spiritual stature and loftiness of this eternal King-Priest, who intercepted Abraham in the Valley of Kings (Shaveh) in Genesis 14. The writer of the Book of Hebrews makes it adamantly clear that the Melchizedek, who intercepted Abraham...

Was a Priest of God Most High

Carried the Blessing of God in His hands

Was the King of Righteousness

Was the King of Peace

You do not have to be a rocket scientist, or an astute theologian, to come to the conclusion that no human being could perfectly fit the above description, other than the Lord Jesus Christ. The Melchizedek, who met Abraham in the Valley of Shaveh, was truly a pre-incarnation appearance of Christ. But, it is what the Apostle Paul tells us about this man, and His eternal priestly Order in Hebrews 7:3 that contain the most potent antidote to the healing of all types of Generational and genetic anomalies. Here is what the Apostle Paul tells us about this heavenly man...

He has no earthly father or mother

He is without a traceable human genealogy

He has no beginning of days or end of life

His priesthood is everlasting

It is clear that in Hebrews 7:3, the Apostle Paul (who was the primary custodian on the revelation on "Christ"), was not referring to Jesus (Yeshua), but to Christ. The name Jesus Christ is the most powerful spiritual technology on earth that carries the divine methodology for how God can appear in the flesh. In my book <u>The Order of Melchizedek</u> I talk about the dichotomy of Jesus Christ, based upon Isaiah 9:6. Isaiah 9:6 tells us that "Jesus" (Yeshua) was the "Child who was born" and "Christ" was the "Son" who was given. Jesus (Yeshua) refers to our Savior's humanity whereas "Christ" refers to our Savior's divinity. In His divinity as the Living Word "Christ" has no earthly father or mother. He has no traceable human genealogy, and He certainly has no beginning of days or end of life. In His divinity, He is also an everlasting High Priest after the Order of Melchizedek.

Since Christ has no earthly genealogy, our marriage to him offers us the best platform for annihilating generational curses that were attached to our natural bloodline. The institution of marriage is based upon inheritance law. When a woman gets married, both her status and her inheritance change. This change in inheritance is signified by the change from her maiden name to that of her new husband. If this is true in the natural, it is also true spiritually. As the Bride of Christ, our marriage to Him forms the legal basis for the complete overhaul of all generational curses against us.

Denouncing our Natural Lineage for the Melchizedek Order

For this Melchisedec, king of Salem, priest of the most high God, who met Abraham returning from the slaughter of the kings, and blessed him; To whom also Abraham gave a tenth part of all; first being by interpretation King of righteousness, and after that also King of Salem, which is, King of peace; Without father, without mother, without descent, having neither beginning of days, nor end of life; but made like unto the Son of God; abideth a priest continually.

Hebrews 7:1-3 KJV

Once we become aware of what Christ has made available to us through his Melchizedek order we need to take the final leap of faith into our inheritance. This final leap of faith involves our willingness to denounce our allegiance to our natural lineage or ancestry line. When a woman gets married, one of the immediate changes that happens in her life is that she gives up her maiden name to embrace her husband's name. For instance if a woman was called Mary Jones when she was single and then she ends up marrying Thomas Jackson; her new name will be "Mary Jackson." Her changed name symbolizes the fact that she has inherited her husband's lineage.

But let us suppose that Mary Jones refuses to take on her husband's name after their marriage; what message is her action sending to her husband? The message is loud and clear; Mary Jones has no desire to be connected to her husband's lineage. By this one action Mary Jones also disinherits herself from the benefits of being part of her husband's lineage. The Holy Spirit told me that this is exactly what the Body of Christ has been doing, when we celebrate our natural lineage at the expense of who we are in Christ.

Whenever I am holding a deliverance service for members of the body of Christ who desire to be set free from the tyranny of generational curses; I lead them through a prayer of renunciation. In this prayer of renunciation they willingly and joyfully renounce their loyalty to their natural lineage in favor of Christ's uncorrupted prophetic bloodline. When people joyfully and willingly do this; we have seen some amazing miracles take place.

LIFE APPLICATION SECTION

MEMORY VERSE

After Abram returned from his victory over Kedorlaomer and all his allies, the king of Sodom went out to meet him in the valley of Shaveh (that is, the King's Valley). And Melchizedek, the king of Salem and a priest of God Most High, brought Abram some bread and wine. Melchizedek blessed Abram with this blessing: "Blessed be Abram by God Most High, Creator of heaven and earth. And blessed be God Most High, who has defeated your enemies for you." Then Abram gave Melchizedek a tenth of all the goods he had recovered.

Genesis 14:17-20

REFLECTIONS

What is the Order of Melchizedek?

_____
_____
_____
_____
_____

How does the Order of Melchizedek facilitate our deliverance from Generational Curses?

_____
_____
_____
_____
_____

JOURNAL YOUR THOUGHTS ON THIS CHAPTER

Chapter Ten

How to Retire Generational Curses Permanently

Though I might also have confidence in the flesh. If any other man thinketh that he hath whereof he might trust in the flesh, I more: Circumcised the eighth day, of the stock of Israel, of the tribe of Benjamin, an Hebrew of the Hebrews; as touching the law, a Pharisee; Concerning zeal, persecuting the church; touching the righteousness which is in the law, blameless. But what things were gain to me, those I counted loss for Christ. Yea doubtless, and I count all things but loss for the excellency of the knowledge of Christ Jesus my Lord: for whom I have suffered the loss of all things, and do count them but dung, that I may win Christ,

Philippians 3:4-8 KJV

During the course of this writing, I have stated that the primary purpose for writing the book was to help the body of Christ gain access to a spiritual technology for breaking generational curses, and reversing genetic anomalies permanently. I'm glad that we have finally got to the chapter where I can show you how to do this, based upon what the Holy Spirit showed me. I don't know about you, but I would not like to go to a doctor for the same ailment all the days of my life. If a doctor really knows what he's doing, he should be able to come up with a permanent solution to what ails me. Jesus Christ is by far the best doctor or physician in human history. This is because the Bible tells us that all things were made by Him and for Him.

In Philippians 3:4-8 the Apostle Paul opens a window into how Kingdom Citizens or "Born again Believers" can break free of the demonic technologies that are attached to their natural lineage or bloodline. In this passage from the

Book of Philippians, the Apostle Paul also gives us a very powerful definition for the flesh. Paul's definition, of the flesh, is very different to what most of us would consider to be the "flesh." Most believers confuse the works of the flesh that Apostle Paul lists in the Book of Galatians in the fifth chapter. But, according to Philippians 3:4-8, "the flesh" and "the works of the flesh" are not the same.

"The works of the flesh" are like the fruit of a tree, whereas "the flesh" is the root system of the tree. A dear friend of mine once told me the following: "If you change the root, you change the fruit." This means that you can never change the fruit of any tree, if you are unwilling to change the root. That is because the life of any tree is found in the root system. With this understanding, let us now examine Philippians 3:4-8 and discover the true meaning of the flesh. The apostle Paul begins presenting this passage by saying that if any man feels like he can have confidence in the flesh, then he was no match for Paul.

The Apostle Paul then lists the following things that he considered to be flesh:

- *His pride over being circumcised the eighth day, (this represents religious pride)*
- *His pride at being of the stock of Israel, (this represents the pride of nationality)*
- *His pride of being of the tribe of Benjamin, (this represents tribal pride)*
- *His pride at being a Hebrew of the Hebrews; (this represents family pedigree)*
- *His religious fervor as touching the law, a Pharisee; (this represents the pride of social status)*
- *Concerning zeal, persecuting the church; (this represents religious zeal without knowledge)*
- *Touching the righteousness which is in the law, blameless; (this represents self righteousness)*

I want you to note that everything that the Apostle Paul lists above are the very things that most believers (including spiritual leaders) fight to maintain. For instance, being proud that you are a Baptist or a Charismatic Believer at the expense of what you are in Christ, is an example of religious pride. The Apostle Paul calls this type of behavior "flesh." When I used to live in Africa, I talked to many Brothers in Christ who were more proud of the tribe that they where born in, than they were proud of being the New Creation.

When I moved from Zambia to South Africa in 1994; I was ushered into a nation of people who were deeply divided over issues of race. In that nation, many worshipped their race or pedigree and were willing to kill the other race or pedigree to prove their point. This demonically engineered fight for national pride, or pedigree, was also very prevalent in the church. Even among the whites themselves there was a deep divide. The divide was between the whites (Caucasians) from England and the whites (Afrikaners) from the Netherlands, who were of Dutch descent. These divisions, over pedigree, were so entrenched into the conscience of the nation that they affected the church deeply. For instance, if you were an English-speaking Born-again Believer (and you happened to visit a Christian church that was led by a pastor who preached in Afrikaans), he would never speak to you in English, even though he could.

Everything that the Apostle Paul lists in Philippians 3:4-8, is historically what has led to many wars and cultural divides over many centuries. But, it is not possible for us to be set free permanently, from generational curses and genetic anomalies, if we are too proud of who we are in the natural apart from who we are in Christ. Everything that the Apostle Paul lists in Philippians 3:4-8 is available to every human being apart from Christ. In other words, you do not need to be in Christ what you already are in the natural. And yet, if we do not count "as loss" everything that we were before God placed us in Christ, we can never find the complete freedom that we seek. Ongoing and permanent freedom from generational curses, and genetic anomalies, will elude us if we do not stop worshiping who we are in the natural.

Hiding Behind the Family Tree

At that moment their eyes were opened, and they suddenly felt shame at their nakedness. So they sewed fig leaves together to cover themselves. When the cool evening breezes were blowing, the man and his wife heard the Lord God walking about in the garden. So they hid from the Lord God among the trees. Then the Lord God called to the man, "Where are you?"

Genesis 3:7-9

Since the fall of Adam and Eve in the Garden of Eden, God continues to search for his lost children who are lost behind the family tree. I once watched a movie in which a married man, who was deeply in love with his wife and children, had a terrible accident. The paramedics could not locate his real family. So, at the hospital, he was addressed as Mr. Unknown. When he came out of his comma, the doctors quickly realized that he had amnesia and suffered a complete loss of his memory. He could not remember his lovely wife or children at all.

While he was in the hospital a nurse befriended him. As she was nursing him back to health, they fail in love. When he got out of the hospital he moved in with her. In the meantime, this man's loving wife and children had put out a missing person report, in his original state of residence. When the police finally located him, they called his wife and children to tell them the good news. This man's wife and his children were overjoyed at the fact that he was not dead. As the story goes this man's wife flew to the town were her husband was living with the nurse who had nursed him back to health.

When this man's real wife finally got to him, their reunion was very complicated to say the least, because the man could not remember her. He welcomed her with deep cautiousness. But, the man's wife had come with her family's photo album. She showed her husband, who could not remember, the photos that they had taken together. After a while, the man began to remember who he was. Slowly but surely, his memory returned. He began to remember the love that he had once shared with the one who was quoting herself to be his wife, and the children that they had together. As this man's memory returned, they brought with them an avalanche of deep-seated emotions of love towards his first family. The nurse (who had nursed him back to health), even though she was still in love with him, knew that she had to let him go. She knew that she could not hold him in the present, when he had remembered who he was. I really believe that this is exactly what God desires to do for the Body of Christ; to help us remember who we are in Christ, and reconnect ourselves to Christ's prophetic bloodline.

Overturning the Power of Inheritance Law

Know ye not, brethren, (for I speak to them that know the law,) how that the law hath dominion over a man as long as he liveth? For the woman which hath an husband is bound by the law to her husband so long as he liveth; but if the husband be dead, she is loosed from the law of her husband. So then if, while her husband liveth, she be married to another man, she shall be called an adulteress: but if her husband be dead, she is free from that law; so that she is no adulteress, though she be married to another man. Wherefore, my brethren, ye also are become dead to the law by the body of Christ; that ye should be married to another, even to him who is raised from the dead, that we should bring forth fruit unto God.

Romans 7:1-4

So, how can we be set free from the tyranny of generational curses and genetic anomalies? I am glad that you asked me. We have to overturn the Power of Inheritance Law over our lives. In Romans 7:1-4, the Apostle Paul lists the spiritual technology for overturning *"The Power of Inheritance Law."* The apostle Paul tells us that the "Law" has dominion over a person as long as he or she lives. Paul goes on to say that a woman with a husband is bound by the Law to her husband, as long as he lives. But, if the husband dies, that woman is loosed from the "Law" of her husband. Paul goes on to say that while her husband is still living, a woman who marries another man shall be called an adulteress. But, if her husband is dead, she is free to marry another husband. Paul then hit the homerun when he finally said that Born-again Believers have died to their first husband (the old nature and its deeds), in order to marry Christ.

Let us now breakdown the prophetic implications of what the apostle Paul is alluding to in Romans 7:1-4. Please bear in mind that we have already concluded that the "flesh" represents everything that we were apart from Christ (which includes our natural lineage or heritage). The Bible also calls the "flesh" the "old man." Let us assume that the husband the Apostle Paul is alluding to in Romans 7:1-4, is the "old man or our "old nature." While we were married to our "old nature" the "Law of sin and death" had complete dominion over us.

Coincidentally, the "Law of sin and death" is the same law that governs every life form in the universe that is under the power of sin. This means that the "Law of sin and death" is the primary law that governs generational curses and genetic anomalies. For as long as we stay married to our first husband ("the old man and his deeds"), the "Law of sin and death" will continue to have dominion over us. The word dominion simply means "to rule" something. We must remember that everything that we where apart from Christ, which includes our lineage, is part and parcel of our "old unregenerate nature." What is adamantly clear is that we cannot be married to two husbands at the same time. A married woman, who is married to another man before she is legally released from her first marriage, is called an adulteress. Many believers for the most part are guilty of committing spiritual adultery; because, they walk in the flesh then flip back to walking in the spirit.

Marriage to Christ: Our Freedom

So then if, while her husband liveth, she be married to another man, she shall be called an adulteress: but if her husband be dead, she is free from that law; so that she is no adulteress, though she be married to another man. Wherefore, my brethren, ye also are become dead to the law by the body of Christ; that ye should be married to another, even to him who is raised from the dead, that we should bring forth fruit unto God.

Romans 7:3-4

When we get to Romans 7:3-4 the Apostle Paul finalizes the technology of our rescue, from the tyranny of Generational Curses and genetic anomalies. The solution to our complete deliverance (that can overturn and reverse the power of inheritance law in our favor), stares us in the face. Our marriage to Christ offers us the ultimate solution, after we choose to put to death our "old nature" (our first husband).

The institution of marriage is the fastest way to change the inheritance of any human being. A woman or man may be living in abject poverty but should they marry a rich spouse, they immediately become wealthy too, from the minute they say, "I do." The Apostle Paul tells us that if we die to the flesh, which was our first husband, the "Law of sin and death" has no power over us. We are free to marry "another" and that "another" in the passage from Romans is "Christ Jesus."

Denouncing your Natural Lineage

Therefore if any man be in Christ, he is a new creature: old things are passed away; behold, all things are become new.

2 Corinthians 5:17 KJV

But what things were gain to me, those I counted loss for Christ.

Philippians 3:7

So how do we benefit the most from our marriage to Christ? To benefit the most from our union with Christ, we must do what every single woman does when she gets married. She legally and joyfully denounces her last name/maiden name (or lineage), in order to take on her husband's name (or lineage).

If the woman's name was Cindy Dunstun when she was single (then she married Matthew Kennedy), she immediately became Cindy Kennedy. This is why, at the end of the wedding vows, the wedding minister turns to the crowd of witnesses and makes this announcement: "I now present to you Mr. and Mrs. Kennedy." The crowd of witness cheers and no one at the wedding ceremony mourns the loss of the woman's last name because it was to be expected; it was the right thing to do. But, why does the Body of Christ hang onto their "old name" (old nature), even though they are married to Christ?

When the Lord revealed to me the technology for breaking Generational Curses (that is contained in this book), He told me that I had to take His Bride (the Body of Christ) through a spiritual ceremony of renunciation. In this ceremony, God's people get an opportunity to legally denounce their allegiance to their natural lineage, in order to embrace their full inheritance as the Bride of Christ. The Lord showed me that based upon Hebrews 7:3, the genealogy of any human bloodline or lineage is rooted in two very powerful people in every person's life, their "Father" and "Mother." This means that all "Generational Curses and Genetic Anomalies" are based upon our mother and father's bloodlines. This fact alone is what makes the "Order of Melchizedek" very valuable to humans who are challenged by demonic interference in our compromised bloodlines. Melchizedek (who is our Lord Jesus Christ)...in His divinity...has "no genealogy" then, in His humanity, Yeshua has a "genetically flawless bloodline."

Based upon our conclusions in the last passage, it is clear that our spiritual inheritance in our marriage to the Lord Jesus Christ is truly priceless. Our marriage to Christ is the antidote that will set us free from the poison of demonic influence in our bloodline. But, we cannot enjoy this incredible blessing if we are unwilling to denounce our natural lineage in favor of "Christ's Melchizedek Order." We must be willing to denounce our allegiance to our natural bloodlines in order to inherit the "genetically flawless bloodline" of our Lord Jesus Christ.

Becoming an Ambassador to your Family

And they said, Is not this Jesus, the son of Joseph, whose father and mother we know? How is it then that he saith, I came down from heaven?

John 6:42

The Lord told me to lead His people through a prayer of renunciation, before I prayed for the complete divine annihilation of any and all generational curses and genetic anomalies attached to their natural bloodlines. The Lord told me that the people have to renounce their allegiance to their "father's and mother's lineage." When the Holy Spirit showed me this, I wanted to know (from the Lord) if this action meant that the people were denouncing their natural families, because I know that God is a God of the family. The Lord assured me that denouncing our natural lineage, in order to embrace His holy prophetic bloodline, does not translate into denouncing our commitment and love for the families that He has given us.

But, the Lord showed me that "denouncing our natural lineage" to embrace our marriage to Christ actually elevates our spiritual stature, before our natural families. This spiritual act of denunciation actually elevates us to become "Kingdom Ambassadors" to our natural family members. The Holy Spirit asked me a question; "What do you call an official who represents his government (Kingdom) on foreign soil?" "An Ambassador" came the answer. The Holy Spirit showed me that God's children have a choice to either be counted as a "mere member" of their natural family or as an "Ambassador" of God's Kingdom to their family. The Holy Spirit showed me that an Ambassador is the only person who can live on foreign soil, and be completely immune to the threats that reside in that country. In the context of this book, if we choose to become Ambassadors of the Kingdom to our families (as opposed to being counted in their numbers), God will make sure that we are "immunized" from any "Generational Curses and Genetic anomalies" that may be running rampart in our natural family.

The Prayer of Renunciation

Below is the prayer that the Holy Spirit gave me for taking any person through complete deliverance, from all "Generational Curses and Genetic Anomalies." Please feel free to read it aloud, if you are trusting God for your own deliverance.

"Heavenly Father, I come boldly before your Throne of Grace. Your Word says that if we confess our sins, you are faithful and just to forgive us our sins and cleanse us from all unrighteousness. I repent for worshipping my family tree, instead of celebrating my position in Christ as the new creation. Heavenly Father, I stand in Your presence and that of your angels, to joyfully and willfully denounce....................(here you insert your father's name to identify your natural lineage) and everything demonic that is attached to the lineage that this name represents (in favor of Christ's Melchizedek Order). Heavenly Father, I stand in your presence and that of your angels, to joyfully and willfully denounce....................(this time you insert your mother's maiden name to identify your natural lineage) and everything demonic that is attached to the lineage that this name represents (in favor of Christ's Melchizedek Order). Heavenly Father, I also beseech you to heal any and all genetic anomalies in my bloodline, by superimposing Yeshua's flawless prophetic bloodline over my own. Thank you for healing me from any and all genetic deficiencies, in the name of Jesus Christ. Amen

Jumping over the Prophetic Bloodline

The final step in this process of deliverance is to jump over a prophetic bloodline that represents the convergence of our father and mother's bloodlines. When the Lord Jesus Christ was downloading the spiritual technology for breaking generational curses that is contained in this book, He showed me a vision of a person standing in front of a line and then jumping over it. I asked the Lord what that meant. The Lord told me that the line on the ground was a prophetic enactment of the natural bloodlines that His people had to jump over, in order to be fully identified with His holy prophetic bloodline.

The Lord told me that after the prayer of renunciation, I was to instruct the recipients of deliverance to jump over the line as a prophetic act. That act symbolized the fact that they were abandoning their allegiance from their natural lineages, to embrace Yeshua's holy prophetic bloodline or generation. The Lord also instructed me to inform deliverance recipients to go into deep and heartfelt praises for the Lord, once they jumped over the line.

While deliverance recipients are praising the Lord, the Lord instructed me to use this time to rebuke demonic powers that were attached to the natural lineages that they had just denounced. I also use this time to ask the Holy Spirit to heal all the genetic anomalies of the deliverance recipients. We have seen the Lord heal genetically induced diseases during these times of prayer. The twelfth chapter of this book includes testimonials of some of the deliverance recipients that I have prayed for. But, any believer can achieve the same results if they simply follow the spiritual protocol that I have laid down in this chapter.

LIFE APPLICATION SECTION

MEMORY VERSE

Though I might also have confidence in the flesh. If any other man thinketh that he hath whereof he might trust in the flesh, I more: Circumcised the eighth day, of the stock of Israel, of the tribe of Benjamin, an Hebrew of the Hebrews; as touching the law, a Pharisee; Concerning zeal, persecuting the church; touching the righteousness which is in the law, blameless. But what things were gain to me, those I counted loss for Christ. Yea doubtless, and I count all things but loss for the excellency of the knowledge of Christ Jesus my Lord: for whom I have suffered the loss of all things, and do count them but dung, that I may win Christ,

Philippians 3:4-8 KJV

REFLECTIONS

How does the Apostle define the "flesh?"

_____
_____
_____
_____
_____

What is a Lineage?

_____
_____
_____
_____
_____

JOURNAL YOUR THOUGHTS ON THIS CHAPTER

Chapter Eleven

THE GENERATIONAL BLESSING

You must not bow down to them or worship them, for I, the Lord your God, am a jealous God who will not tolerate your affection for any other gods. I lay the sins of the parents upon their children; the entire family is affected, even children in the third and fourth generations of those who reject me. ***But I lavish unfailing love for a thousand generations on those who love me and obey my commands.***

Exodus 20:5-6 KJV

Even though this book is about the return of an ancient spiritual technology for overturning "Generational curses and genetic anomalies;" I would be amiss to end it on that note. I want this book to draw the attention of the body of Christ towards what God desires His people to experience, after we are delivered from generational curses and genetic anomalies. God desires to help us break through the barrier of "Generational curses" into the refreshing Streams of the "Generational blessing."

Most spiritual leaders (who teach on breaking "Generational curses") are so focused on breaking these curses that they do not stop to meditate on Exodus 20:6. The first five verses in the 20th chapter of Exodus addresses the spiritual consequences of our disobedience to God. But the sixth verse is very telling, as to God's primary agenda for warning us against participating in the demonic activity, mentioned in the prior verses. God's intention is to bring His people into the "Generational blessing."

What is of note is that "Generational curses" can go up to the third and fourth generation but, the "Generational blessing" can last up to a thousand generations. Imagine a blessing so powerful that it can last up to a thousand lifetimes. Some of us cannot even imagine that such a blessing is even possible.

Imagine a "Generational blessing" that can guarantee that in a thousand lifetimes our descendants will still be enjoying the blessing of the Almighty God. This is what the Lord desires for his people to come into.

Naboth's Vineyard

Now there was a man named Naboth, from Jezreel, who owned a vineyard in Jezreel beside the palace of King Ahab of Samaria. One day Ahab said to Naboth, "Since your vineyard is so convenient to my palace, I would like to buy it to use as a vegetable garden. I will give you a better vineyard in exchange, or if you prefer, I will pay you for it." But Naboth replied, "The Lord forbid that I should give you the inheritance that was passed down by my ancestors."

1 Kings 21:1-3

So Ahab went home angry and sullen because of Naboth's answer. The king went to bed with his face to the wall and refused to eat!5 "What's the matter?" his wife Jezebel asked him. "What's made you so upset that you're not eating?"6 "I asked Naboth to sell me his vineyard or trade it, but he refused!" Ahab told her. 7 "Are you the king of Israel or not?" Jezebel demanded. "Get up and eat something, and don't worry about it. I'll get you Naboth's vineyard!"

1 Kings 21:4-7

God is a God who loves to see his people come into their inheritance. This is evidenced in the Scriptures by how God defends the disinherited. The primary reason why God destroyed the nation of Egypt during the days of Moses was because the Egyptians had denied the people of Israel a pathway into their inheritance. They made them work many hours building the pyramids of Egypt, without any pathway to obtaining their own inheritance. This grieved and angered the heart of God, who is the God of the inheritance. He is the God of the generational blessing.

In the book of 1 Kings 21:1-3 we have a very interesting story about an issue concerning an inheritance. King Ahab, the husband of the wicked woman Jezebel, wanted to buy the vineyard of one of his subjects by the name of Naboith. King Ahab offered to buy the vineyard belonging to Naboith for more money than it was worth but, Naboith refused to sell it to him. Naboith's reason for refusing to honor the king's request was because the vineyard was priceless to him. It was the inheritance of his forefathers. This particular vineyard had been in his family for many generations. The vineyard had become a symbol of something money cannot buy. Also, the vineyard had become over time a family heirloom, and he could not part with it for any amount of money.

Jezebel's Greatest Mistake

So Ahab went home angry and sullen because of Naboth's answer. The king went to bed with his face to the wall and refused to eat!5 "What's the matter?" his wife Jezebel asked him. "What's made you so upset that you're not eating?"6 "I asked Naboth to sell me his vineyard or trade it, but he refused!" Ahab told her.7 "Are you the king of Israel or not?" Jezebel demanded. "Get up and eat something, and don't worry about it. I'll get you Naboth's vineyard!" 1 Kings 21:4-7

When King Ahab got to his palace, a cloud of depression was plastered all over his face. His conniving wife Jezebel asked him to tell her what was wrong with him. He proceeded to tell her about his conversation with Naboith, over the sale of his vineyard. Jezebel responded with undisguised contempt for the King. She told him that he was acting like a fool, instead of acting like a King. She promised him that she would get the vineyard from Naboth's possession.

Jezebel proceeded to write letters to the nobles, and palace officials, who lived in Naboith's city. She sent them letters on the King's letterhead, bearing his royal signature. In her letter, Jezebel instructed the nobles to invite Naboith to a prestigious meal with the Leaders of the city. She also instructed them to hire the services of two professional liars, and instruct them to bring up a false accusation against Naboith, while they were eating. These nobles were terrified of Jezebel and did exactly as she asked. When Naboith came to attend a state dinner, these professional liars rose against him and began to accuse him of treason.

Since treason was an offense punishable with death, these nobles (who had entered into a conspiracy with Jezebel to kill Naboith), persuaded the people to stone Naboith. After Naboith was stoned to death, these nobles sent a message to Jezebel to inform her that the mission had been accomplished. Jezebel then went to her husband and told him that he could have Naboith's vineyard, because Naboith was dead. King Ahab got into his royal chariots and rushed to Naboith's vineyard to possess it. While he was inspecting Naboith's vineyard, God sent the prophet Elijah with a word of judgment that marked the beginning of the end, for the wicked woman Jezebel. This time, Jezebel had gone too far. She had incensed the heart of a holy God for killing an innocent man who was only trying to defend his inheritance, or the generational blessing that his forefathers left him.

The moral of this story is, even though Jezebel was a wicked queen and had committed great sins against the Lord, it was her conspiracy to kill Naboith over the inheritance of his forefathers that broke the Carmel's back. God had enough of Jezebel's wickedness. She signed her own death warrant, when she shed the blood of an innocent man over his inheritance.

Jezebel's Judgment

And regarding Jezebel, the Lord says, 'Dogs will eat Jezebel's body at the plot of land in Jezreel.

1 Kings 21:23

The prophet Elijah proceeded to pronounce judgment on Jezebel, because of her involvement in the death of Naboith. The prophet Elijah prophesied that God was going to make sure that Jezebel's death would be as inhumane as the death that she had dished out to Naboith. The prophet Elijah prophesied that dogs would eat Jezebel's body, just like the dogs had eaten the body of Naboith. In accordance with the Prophet Elijah's prophecy, Jezebel died a very horrible death. When Jehu became a king over Israel, he commanded the eunuch's who took care of Jezebel, to throw her out of a window. The Eunuch's listened to him, and was empowered by Jehu's voice to throw her out of the window. She fell to the ground, where her body broke into several pieces, and the dogs of the city gathered around her body and began to eat it. She died exactly like the innocent man she had killed, over his inheritance. This story does confirm the fact that God wants his people to experience the "Generational blessing."

The Generational Blessing

Christ hath redeemed us from the curse of the law, being made a curse for us: for it is written, Cursed is every one that hangeth on a tree: That the blessing of Abraham might come on the Gentiles through Jesus Christ; that we might receive the promise of the Spirit through faith.

Galatians 3:13-14 KJV

In the above passage of Scripture, the Apostle Paul makes it very clear that Christ died on the cross, to redeem us from the curse of the law, so the blessing of Abraham might come upon the Gentiles. What is interesting about this passage of Scripture is that it goes beyond the religious understanding of why Jesus Christ was crucified. If you ask most people why Jesus Christ was crucified, they will quickly tell you that it was to pay for our sins. Without a doubt this is true. But, it focuses our attention on the negative side of redemption, and fails to acknowledge the positive side of redemption. The negative side of redemption focuses on the removal of sin. The positive side of redemption focuses on the benefits of righteousness that God wants to bestow upon us, in Christ Jesus. Armed with this knowledge, the Apostle Paul tells us that Christ died on the cross, so the blessing that was upon Abraham might come upon the Gentiles. In other words, the Lord Jesus Christ died on the cross not only to pay for our sins, but to also secure the "Generational blessing" for all of God's children.

LIFE APPLICATION SECTION

MEMORY VERSE

So Ahab went home angry and sullen because of Naboth's answer. The king went to bed with his face to the wall and refused to eat! "What's the matter?" his wife Jezebel asked him. "What's made you so upset that you're not eating?" "I asked Naboth to sell me his vineyard or trade it, but he refused!" Ahab told her. "Are you the king of Israel or not?" Jezebel demanded. "Get up and eat something, and don't worry about it. I'll get you Naboth's vineyard!"

1 Kings 21:4-7

REFLECTIONS

What was Jezebel's greatest sin that led to her death?
___
___
___
___
___

What is a Generational Blessing?
___

JOURNAL YOUR THOUGHTS ON THIS CHAPTER

BREAKING GENERATIONAL CURSES UNDER THE ORDER OF MELCHIZEDEK

Chapter
Twelve

TESTIMONIAL CASE STUDIES

I have always believed that every technology whether it be natural or spiritual needs to be tested before it is exported to the end user. After the Lord gave me the revelation that is contained in this book, I asked Him to give me opportunities to prove the credibility of this technology in undeniable results. God did not disappoint. Since I started praying for His people in accordance with the revelation contained in this writing the results have been very satisfying. This chapter is a collection of a few of the many testimonies that we have received since we started exporting this technology on deliverance from "Generational Curses" to the end user.

Beth El's testimony

It all started in June of 2009 when there was an invasion from heaven without warning in my bedroom. I had a visitation from the King of Kings. He walked like a lion in my room from the Spirit realm towards me face to face. His robe was the most incredible, beautiful white I had ever seen and we didn't speak but He knew my thoughts and I stood still and felt His presence and His love surround me. He had the most tender look on His face and yet a boldness at the same time. I cannot go on with details but clearly it transformed my life because He intercepted me from myself.

Not till October 2010 did I begin to understand the fullness of His intention and interception. It was the revelation that God had given Dr. Francis Myles with which I am eternally grateful for him. Much has transpired since then on my journey with the Lord. I moved from New York City in May of 2010 (the east), to Sedona, Arizona (the west). I traveled from the concrete jungle of Manhattan, New York to the red rock mountains of Sedona.

I was invited to a meeting called The Kingdom, Power & Glory Festival. David & Stephanie Herzog, Lance Wallnau and Dr. Francis Myles were the speakers there in September of 2010. When Dr. Francis spoke and shared about His book the Spirit of Divine Interception he said this is for someone who really needs this. I was glued to my seat and immediately I jumped up and ran to the front to get his book. Dr. Francis looked at me with a very serious look and said this is the book God wants you to have. When I read page 58 of this book what "divine interception" means " God gets you first before the devil has a chance to take you out". I started to understand what God wanted me to know and why He visited me.

Dr. Francis talked about a cutting edge Leadership University called The Order of Melchizedek that the Lord had given Him and I knew in my spirit I had to go. On October 21-23 of 2010. The greatest change began in my life as I attended the University. Those who are serious to jump the line into the Kingdom MUST do this by faith and enter into Christ in us the hope of Glory.

I acknowledged that Christ as our Melchizedek, King, husband and all established the legal grounds for dismissing all generational curses because Christ has no genealogy.

He had no mother, no father, and no ancestral line, neither with beginning of days nor ending of life. (Hebrews 7:1-3) Soon after the graduation I pondered so many things that Dr. Francis spoke on. Most recently I have seen many answers to prayers rapidly since I jumped the line.

Here is a testimony that happened soon after The Order of Melchizedek Leadership University. Someone gave me a car at my church called Solid Rock in Sedona. It was not the one I asked for but God had a greater plan and I trusted Him. Within three weeks I sold the car with ease and used the monies towards my dream car. The car I desired was in the craigslist by a private owner. No struggle just going with His flow in the know. Through a woman I met in town she told me about an auto mechanic who worked on BMW cars. I called and he checked out the car and he said it is in impeccable condition and low miles. He exclaimed, "what a great price"! There it was so fast. I was so blessed by what He gave me and I cried for joy. I now have a beautiful BMW silver convertible with all the extras. It drives so smooth.

Then Yeshua, (Jesus) reminded me of (Psalm 37:4) Delight yourself in the Lord and He will give you the secret petitions of your heart. The greatest part that was better than getting the car was that I led the woman who owned the car to the Lord! Many more things to tell of what He has done recently but it would fill a large portion of this book.

I have denounced my past natural lineage forever and legally no longer tied to my bloodline. I am established on the eternal pathway with Christ. I desire what God wants for me and choose to serve Him all the days of my life. It all started with the revelation God gave Dr. Francis Myles. What a treasure we have from Dr. Francis Myles and his beautiful wife Trina. Thank you Yeshua. I can see clearly now and desire to continue this journey in obedience to God as the great interceptor.

The Verna B, Testimony

Friday evening Verna B a member of Kingdom Point Ministries; Austin, Texas hobbled into our Austin meeting desperate for healing. For over 12 years rheumatoid arthritis had settled into her right knee and leg so severely she begged the Lord to rip the leg off. On a scale of one to ten the pain maxed out over twenty plus. Removing the leg seemed to be her only option. This is her story:

Pastor Joshua mentioned the upcoming meeting with Dr. Francis Myles. I had lots of bad stuff clinging to my natural lineage but had never found a way to release it. Daily emotional trauma was so devastating even the slightest thing could bring a flood of tears.

My healing came as a result of understanding the message Dr. Myles had come to share with us, "Breaking Generational Curses under the Order of Melchizedek." This is one of the best teachings I have ever heard. WOW, Dr. Myles is truly led by the Lord!

After he finished teaching Dr Francis Myles asked everyone in the Church to stand in front of a line; which he said would be a prophetic representation of our sin ravaged natural lineages. Then he took us through a time of denouncing our allegiances to our natural lineages, in favor of "Yeshua's" prophetic bloodline. After the prayers of renunciation, he told us to jump over the line on the floor representing our natural heritage; while he asked God to destroy every generational curse and infuse us with Christ's prophetic bloodline. Not only is all my pain gone since I jumped over the line, but now I can dance with my poodle Jeremiah. Giving up was not an option and neither was removing my leg. God had a better way and I am truly grateful.

Testimony of a Close Friend

Not too long ago I ministered to dear friends of mine in the privacy of their own home. This family had a long history of generational witchcraft in their bloodline. Even though they were Born Again Believers, and had been for some time, circumstances were still out of balance within their family. For almost 20 years the mother within this family had struggled with the guilt of physically leaving her own childhood family behind, and moving away to have her own life. This is the mother's story:

I have been through years of forgiveness and deliverance. No matter what I did, I was not able to let go of the guilt of leaving my family behind to fend for themselves. It has been quite some time since we physically lived close to my family. As able, we do stay in touch with each other.

y (or at least twice a week), she had been having a recurring frightening dream. Within the dream, the child was at her grandparent's house. Wolves with glaring red eyes were always watching her. The child would fall into a corridor that wound around and dropped into a dark and dreary dungeon. Her grandfather was being held as a passive prisoner within that dungeon. Many people, with various weapons, would gather around those trapped in the dungeon, intending to do them great harm.

Dr. Myles came to our house and began to teach us how to deal with generational curses, to leave the past behind. None of my children were present when Dr. Myles took us through the deliverance of jumping the line. I did not even mention anything on the subject to them.

The following morning our daughter came to share the dream, as she had so many times before. This time things had changed. My daughter was instructed to sing specific songs within the dream. As she did so, a man in the dream that had been intending to cause her harm led her to safety out of the dungeon. Although the grandfather was left in his passive state within the dungeon, my daughter was now free from the torment of her recurring nightmares. My guilt in leaving my family behind is gone and my daughter has not had any more nightmares about being helpless and trapped in a dungeon.

Weslyn W Testimony

I absolutely attest to the power and freedom my life has received through this teaching by Dr. Myles on the Order of Melchizedek. Since jumping the line and cutting off all bondages in my lineage my life has soared in literally every area. I particularly notice the ability to be in tune with hearing God's language. Whereas before I struggled remembering "after the fact" those habits I was trying to break off my life – now I see it coming and duck! There is such a higher "knowing" in my spirit of the Christ who is my Lord and King and a FREEDOM released over my life from the Biblical revelations in this teaching. I am given opportunities to share it with everyone I meet! Praise be to God Most High! Weslyn W, Capstone Prayer Ministries, Inc. CAPSTONE PROGRAM MANAGEMENT, INC. PLANO , TX

Craig Clayton Testimony

As a member of Into His Chamber Ministries International under the spiritual guidance of Apostle Helen and Bishop George Saddler I would like to express my sincere gratitude for your recent visit to the House of the Lord. I have been in the financial industry and the marketplace itself for many years. God has blessed me to own several businesses to date and I have owned many in the past. I say that to say this… My Apostle has always provided us with the kind of leadership and spiritual guidance that has helped us to be fruitful in the marketplace. Her teachings on prosperity and wealth are truly anointed, and when she brought The Order of Melchizedek to IHCM. We finally understood that we were operating at the full extent of our genealogy because of the ties to it. When we disclaimed our lineage and our ties to our family tree it released those of us in the marketplace to a Renaissance Marketplace Anointing connected only to our prophetical lineage that allowed us to be completely submersed in the River of GOD. After Dr. Myles left our church, Apostle sent out a series of blessing and prayers through text to all of her leaders. It was intense and filled with power as it outlined our success under the order of Melchizedek. At the time I was going through a military security clearance evaluation, which had been going on for two years. I was at home when the first one came through and immediately I received a call to come in and fill out the final part of my application. I was overwhelmed at how the knowledge of The Order of Melchizedek and operating in the same are so different. Upon my arrival there at the Security Office I was waiting in line when the Chief of Security who happened to walk by greeted me and she invited me to her office to take care of me. While sitting there the second Order of Melchizedek text from Apostle came through stating that immediate and uncommon favor would be ours as we embraced the Order of Melchizedek through Jesus Christ. Before

I could get back to my car the last text came through outlining the measure of success of our prophetic lineage. My phone rang it was the Chief of Security saying that she had spoken with the Chief of Security for the Army in D.C. and my clearance would be approved immediately. When you are in the River of God the struggle becomes the opposite because the River is the very will of God and there is no struggle in Him. His word had already prophetically been spoken that I would be granted my security clearance and that I would be promoted to Master Sergeant. Jesus Christ is our Lord and Savior and Under the Order of Melchizedek we see the outline and the blueprint for navigating this worldly maze as the Lord has the final word over our lives.

Chapter
Thirteen

THE 12 ANCIENT OILS OF SCRIPTURE

But my people are not so reliable, for they have deserted me; they burn incense to worthless idols. They have stumbled off the ancient highways and walk in muddy paths.
Jeremiah 18:15

In the first chapter of this book I dedicated an entire chapter to introduce to the importance of the ancient pathways. We are living in a great time in human history when God is restoring the ancient paths and the wisdom of the ancients. It is a great time to be alive indeed. At this juncture I want to introduce you to one of my students and business partner, Teri Secrest.

Teri Secrest is a woman of God, who loves the Order of Melchizedek and the Kingdom of God. She carries a strong passion to see God's people get back their health by rediscovering the ancient oils of scripture and their healing properties. Since this is a book about totaling healing and deliverance through rediscovering the ancient pathways of God, I felt it was appropriate to introduce my readers to the healing powers of the twelve ancient oils of scripture.

Teri Secrest is also one of my personal wellness coaches and I have asked her to bless my readers by giving them a "live personal wellness consultation" if they call and reference my book. At the end of Teri's presentation of the twelve ancient oils of scripture she will give you a number that you can call to get your free consultation.

Please remember that to take advantage of this offer you have to call and then say that you got the information and telephone number from the book, "Breaking Generational Curses under the Order of Melchizedek."

Yours for Kingdom Advancement

Dr. Francis Myles

Experiencing the
12 Oils of Ancient Scripture

*Written by
Teri Secrest
&
Cristina
Campbell*

Plants have been given to us on the Third Day of Creation

"The earth brought forth vegetation, plants yielding seed after their kind, and trees bearing fruit with seed in them, after their kind; and God saw that it was good. There was evening and there was morning, a third day."

Genesis 1:12-13

Essential Oils were the Oils used for Healing

"Oil for the light, spices for anointing oil, and for sweet incense"

Exodus 25:6

In Biblical times essential oils were often mixed in a vegetable oil base such as olive, flaxseed, walnut, sesame, or almond. But vegetable oils alone were never used for anointing. In fact, the word "anointment" is literally "an ointment". Biblical ointments were always composed of essential oils.

Except from "The healing Oils of the Bible" by David Stewart

The Biblical Meaning of Anointing

The Hebrew word for "anoint" is *masach*, which means "to smear, spread, or massage," and in some cases it means "to pour oil over the head or body." This is no small amount of oil. ...precious was never applied to olive oil alone, but always indicated the use of oils such as cassia, hyssop, and frankincense...

Except from "The healing Oils of the Bible" by David Stewart

The Anointing of David

The Anointing of Saul

Then Samuel took a flask of oil and poured it on Saul's head and kissed him, saying, "Has not the LORD anointed you leader over his inheritance?

Samuel 10:1

Thou anointest my head with oil...

Psalm 23

The Anointing of Aaron

"And Moses took the anointing oil... And he poured of the anointing oil upon Aaron's head, and anointed him, to sanctify him."
Leviticus 8:10-12

"It is like the precious ointment upon the head, that ran down upon the beard, even Aaron's beard: that went down to the skirts of his garments."
Psalm 133:2

What are Essential Oils?

The life-blood distilled of aromatic plants

The Immune system of the plant
Liquid gold obtained from the leaves,
flowers, roots, stems of plants
and bark of trees

The Power of Young Living Therapeutic Grade

True essential oil quality starts at the source. Young Living has developed pure, organic farms in Mona, Utah, St. Marie's, Idaho, Simiane-la-Rotonde, France and Guayaquil, Ecuador.

Young Living is the largest distiller of therapeutic grade essential oils today.

We are the world leader in essential oils.

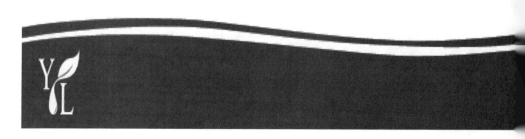

Essential Oils Support all Five Elements of Our Health

When one area of our health gets out of balance, our entire body becomes imbalanced. The **12 Oils of Ancient Scripture** support all 5 areas of our health.

Our Body's Frequency is an important component of our Health

Frequency is the measurable rate of an electrical current from point A to point B. All living matter carries a frequency. A healthy body, from head to foot, typically has a frequency ranging from 62 to 78 MHz, while disease begins at 58 MHz. Essential oils start at 46 MHz and go as high as 320 MHz, which is the frequency of rose oil. Essential oils contain frequencies that are several times greater than the frequencies of herbs and food. This means that essential oils have more life giving energy than any other substance.

- Flu like symptoms at 58 MHz
- Viral Infection at 55 MHz
- Epstein Barr at 52 MHz
- Tissue breakdown from disease at 48 MHz
- Cancer at 42 MHz
- Death begins at 20 MHz

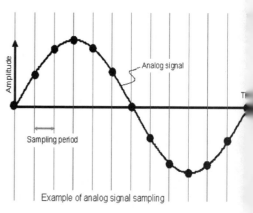

By applying essential oils to our body daily we are protecting our bodies from the onslaught of disease and sickness.

Three Ways to Experience the Scriptural Oils

1. Rub topically on location

2. Diffuse into the air

3. Breathe during prayer time

James 5:14

"Is any sick among you? Let him call for the elders of the church; and let them pray over him, anointing him with oil in the name of the Lord."

Frankincense is a Treasure

"There is **treasure** to be desired and oil in the dwelling of the wise..."

Proverbs 21:20

"...and when they had opened their **treasures**, they presented unto him gifts; gold, and frankincense and myrrh."

Matthew 2:10

Historical Frankincense

- Frankincense is extracted from the Boswellia tree.
- The tree must be 40 years old before even one drop of oil can be extracted. In Biblical times 40 years was considered to be a generation.
- Hebrew and Greek *incense*, is translated to *Frankincense*.
- 52 biblical references to Frankincense

Exodus 30:34
Song of Solomon 3:6; 4:6, 14
Leviticus 2:1, 15, 16; 5:11; 6:15; 24:7
Numbers 5:15
Isaiah 43:23; 60:6; 66:3
1 Chronicles 9:29
Jeremiah 6:20; 17:26; 41:5
Nehemiah 13:5,9
Revelation 18:13

Ancient Boswellia Tree

Exciting Frankincense Research

ecancermedicalscience

Frankincense oil derived from Boswellia carteri induces bladder tumor cell specific cytotoxicity

Date: 18/03/2009

Frankincense oil - a potential treatment option for bladder cancer

An enriched extract of the Somalian Frankincense herb Boswellia carteri has been shown to kill off bladder cancer cells. Frankincense oil is prepared from aromatic hardened gum resins obtained by tapping Boswellia trees. One of the main components of frankincense oil is boswellic acid, a component known to have anti-neoplastic properties. Research presented in the peer reviewed journal, *BMC Complementary and Alternative Medicine* found that ;Frankincense oil might represent an alternative intravesical agent for bladder cancer treatment.

HK Lin and his team, from the University of Oklahoma Health Sciences Center and Oklahoma City VA Medical Center, set out to evaluate frankincense oil for its anti-tumour activity in bladder cancer cells. The authors investigated the effects of the oil in two different types of cells in culture: human bladder cancer cells and normal bladder cells. The team found that frankincense oil is able to discriminate between normal and cancerous bladder cells in culture, and specifically kill cancer cells.

Within a range of concentration, frankincense oil suppressed cell viability in bladder transitional carcinoma J82 cells but not in UROtsa cells. Comprehensive gene expression analysis confirmed that frankincense oil activates genes that are responsible for cell cycle arrest, cell growth suppression, and apoptosis in J82 cells. However, frankincense oil-induced cell death in J82 cells did not result in DNA fragmentation, a hallmark of apoptosis.

Article: Frankincense oil derived from Boswellia carteri induces tumor cell specific cytotoxicity
Mark Barton Frank, Qing Yang, Jeanette Osban, Joseph T Azzarello, Marcia R Saban, Ricardo Saban, Richard A Ashley, Jan C Welter, Kar-Ming Fung and Hsueh-Kung Lin
http://www.biomedcentral.com/bmccomplementalternmed/

© 2009 ecancermedicalscience

- ✓ Suppresses cancer cells
- ✓ Has anti-tumor activity
- ✓ Cancer cell growth suppression
- ✓ Able to discriminate between normal and cancer cells

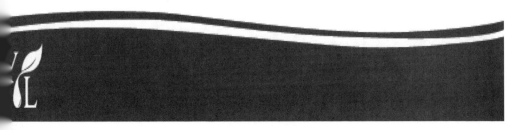

More Frankincense Research
(Boswellia Carteri)

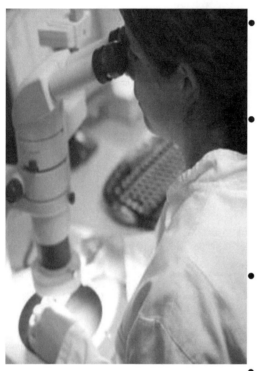

Frankincense oil derived from Boswellia carteri induces tumor cell specific cytotoxicity
BMC Complementary and Alternative Medicine 2009, 9:6 doi:10.1186/1472-6882-9-6
http://www.biomedcentral.com/1472-6882/9/6

- Reverses multiple brain tumors in a breast cancer patient
- Used for the treatment of rheumatoid arthritis and other inflammatory diseases such as Crohn's disease
- Provides protective effects in ulcerative colitis model
- Used in traditional medicine in many other countries.

Modern Uses for Frankincense

- Rub on chest and over lungs for respiratory support

- Breathe deeply for emotional support

- Use for exquisite skin care

- Rub on feet for Immune system support

- Diffuse for overall body support

- Anoint yourself during prayer

Myrrh and the Story of Queen Esther

"...for so were the days of their purifications accomplished, to wit, six months with oil of myrrh, and six months with sweet odours, and with other things for the purifying of the women;)"

Esther 2:12

"And the king loved Esther above all the women, and she obtained grace and favour in his sight more than all the virgins; so that he set the royal crown upon her head, and made her queen instead of Vashti."

Esther 2:17

Queen Esther

More Scriptures on Myrrh

Psalms 45:8 "All thy garments smell of myrrh, and aloes, and cassia, out of the ivory palaces, whereby they have made thee glad."

Proverbs 7:17 "I have perfumed my bed with myrrh, aloes, and cinnamon."

Song of Solomon 5:1 "I am come into my garden, my sister, my spouse: I have gathered my myrrh with my spice;"

- *Genesis 37:25; 43:11*
- *Exodus 30:23; 30: 22, 34*
- *Esther 2:12*
- *Song of Solomon 1:13; 3:6; 4:6; 14; 5:13*
- *Matthew 2:11;*
- *Mark 15:23*
- *John 19:39*

Research on Myrrh
(Commiphora myrrha)

- Myrrh, fragrant resin with ancient heritage, may bear anti-cancer agents
  - Rutgers University Study Dec 6, 2001
- A natural drug to treat pain
- Skin infections
- Inflammatory conditions
- Periodontal diseases
- Antiseptic, anesthetic, and antitumor properties
  - Holist Nurs Pract. 2007 Nov-Dec;21(6):308-23.

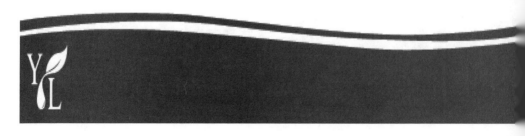

Ancient Uses of Myrrh

- Used as a fixative to prolong the life of the fragrances of perfumes and ointments
- Birthing mothers anointed the umbilical cord for protection against infection
- Used for Oral Hygiene (gingivitis, periodontal disease and cancer sores)
- Diffused and inhaled during labor to reduce anxiety and facilitate calmness
- Used for Skin conditions to prevent abdominal stretch marks
- Insect repellant

Modern uses for Myrrh

- Exquisite Skin Care
- Gingivitis and mouth ulcers
- Rub on chest for viral infections and bronchitis
- Drop on fungal infections
- Apply to cracked lips and wrinkles

(For sensitive skin mix with Young Livings V-6 in the palm of your hand

Myrrh and precancerous skin condition

Carl and Janice Weger Denver, Colorado

"My husband Carl was told by the doctor that he had a precancerous skin condition on his face that should be frozen with liquid nitrogen. Carl had this done once before, and it was expensive. So he asked if we had any essential oils for that. I suggested Myrrh. He applied a couple drops of Myrrh topically on the area once a day for 2 weeks. The area was dry for about 2 weeks, then it totally healed and the condition was reversed.
So we are total believers in the power of Myrrh for skin conditions."

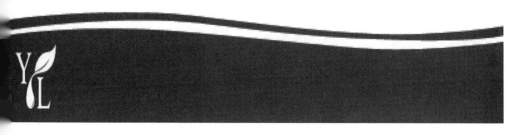

Cedarwood in Scriptures

"And he spake of trees, from the cedar tree that is in Lebanon even unto the hyssop that springeth out of the wall". *1 Kings 4:33*

"The trees of the Lord are full of sap, the cedars of Lebanon, which he hath planted." *Psalms 104:16*

Cedarwood is mentioned 25 times in the Bible, in 8 books of the Bible.

- *Leviticus 14:51, 14:52*
- *Numbers 19:6, 24;6*
- *2 Samuel 5:11, 7:2, 7:7*
- *1 Kings 4:33, 5:6, 5:8, 5:10, 6:9 9:11*
- *2 Kings 19:23*
- *1 Chronicles 22:4,*
- *2 Chronicles 1:15, 2:8, 9:27*
- *Ezra 3:7*
- *Isaiah 41:19*
- *Ezekiel 17:3, 17:22, 17:23*
- *Zechariah 11:2*

Cedarwood Research
(Cedrus Atlantica)

ADD/ADHD - Dr. Terry Friedmann, MD, found in clinical tests that Cedarwood oil was able to successfully treat ADD and ADHD (attention deficit disorders) in children. It is recognized for its calming, purifying properties.

Highest of all oils in sequiterpenes 98% - Studies reveal that Sesquiterpenes in these oils cross the blood brain barrier and oxygenate the pineal and pituitary glands and to stimulate the limbic region of the brain.

Antibacterial - PMID: 16076643 [PubMed - indexed for MEDLINE]

Hair loss - Randomized trial of aromatherapy, Successful treatment for Alopecia Areata. Arch Dermatol. 1998;134 (11):1349-52.

Combats candida - PMID: 14615795 [PubMed - indexed for MEDLINE]

Antifungal – PMID: 14615795 [PubMed - indexed for MEDLINE]

It has also been used to promote **better nerve and kidney function.**

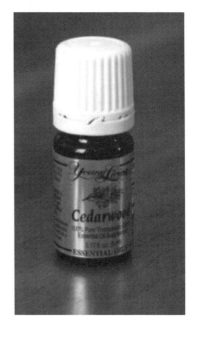

Ancient Uses of Cedarwood

From the mighty "Cedars of Lebanon" came the fragrant and long lasting wood used to build Solomon's temple.

- Spiritual cleansing
- Disinfecting temple instruments
- Cosmetics
- Skin problems
- Calming Effects
- Stimulating the mind and emotional cleansing
- Various Medicines
- Embalming

Modern Uses of Cedarwood

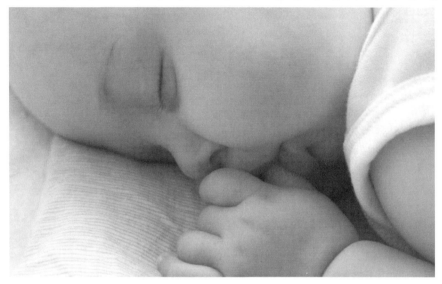

- Calming and grounding on an emotional level
- Great natural insect repellant
- Rub into scalp for thinning hair
- Use for acne and psoriasis
- Use to stimulate the lymph system
- Helps to enhance sleep by increasing melatonin in the brain
- Breathe to promote mental clarity

Biblical Oils come to the Rescue

Carolyn Watts   Doha, Qatar

Recipe:
½ cup of Olive oil
5 drops Myrrh
5 drops sandalwood
5 drops cedarwood
5 drops spikenard

"Since moving to Doha, Qatar, near the Persian gulf. I have become VERY interested in the Oils of Ancient Scripture. After a couple months in the hot, dry weather here I noticed a change in my skin and hair. My hair was falling out and completely changed into dry, brittle hair. It was shocking. So right away I mixed drops of Myrrh, Spikenard, Cedarwood and Sandalwood in a cup of olive oil and covered my hair and scalp with it. After two hours I shampooed my hair and WOW, I couldn't believe the difference! My hair was soft again!

I use this combo once a week on my hair now and it has stopped falling out completely and has become thicker and softer. All my friends here are asking me for my oil treatment now! As for my skin Myrrh and Spikenard are a great addition to my ART skin care for the extra moisture. I am so grateful for Young Living quality oils!"

Cypress in Scripture

Genesis 6:14 "So make yourself an ark of cypress wood; make rooms in it and coat it with pitch inside and out. ... Make yourself a ship of cypress wood..."

Isaiah 14:8 "Indeed the cypress trees rejoice over you, And the cedars of Lebanon, Saying, 'Since you were cut down, No woodsman has come up against us.'"

Isaiah 44:14 "He heweth him down cedars, and taketh the cypress and the oak, which he strengtheneth for himself among the trees of the forest: he planteth an ash, and the rain doth nourish [it]."

1 Kings 9:11 "Hiram the king of Tyre had furnished Solomon with cedar trees and cypress trees, and with gold, according to all his desire,) that then king Solomon gave Hiram twenty cities in the land of Galilee."

Song of Solomon 1:17 "The beams of our house are cedar, and our rafters of fir."

Isaiah 60:13; Ezekiel 27:6; II Chronicles 3:5; I Kings 6:3

Research on Cypress
(Cupressus sempervirens)

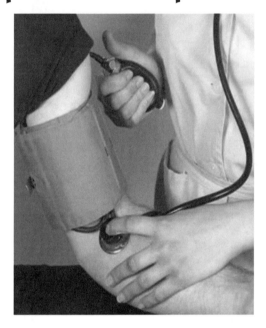

Work carried out by Dr. Gary Schwartz, Professor of Psychology and Psychiatry at Yale University, found that the aromas of some essential oils by themselves reduced blood pressure. Cypress essential oil has been found to be beneficial in the treatment of hypertension.

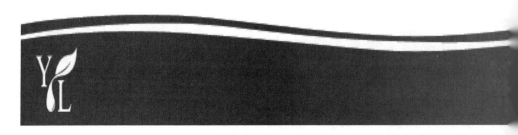

Ancient Uses of Cypress

The doors in St. Peter's cathedral are 1200 years old and are made out of Cypress. They have absolutely no signs of aging, which shows you the durability of Cypress.

Arthritis, laryngitis, reducing scar tissue, cramps

Cypress wood was used for building ships and houses by the ancient Phoenicians and Cretans.

The island of Cyprus was named after it. At this time, the custom of planting Cypress trees in Mediterranean cemeteries, symbolizing life after death began. Even today, many cemeteries around the world are graced with beautiful towering Cypress trees.

Perhaps related to the Hebrew word gopher, name of the tree whose wood was used to make the ark *(Gen. vi.14).*

Modern Uses of Cypress

- Helps support bones and connective tissue
- Improves circulation
- Helps to lessen scar tissue
- Increases white blood cells
- Reduces swelling from edema
- Strengthens your teeth and gums
- Diffuse to ease feelings of loss
- Strengthens blood capillaries

Sandalwood/Aloes in Scriptures

"All Your garments are scented with myrrh and *aloes* and cassia, out of the ivory palaces, by which they have made You glad."
Psalms 45:8

"I have perfumed my bed with myrrh, aloes, and cinnamon."
Proverbs 7:17

"And there came also Nicodemus, which at the first came to Jesus by night, and brought a mixture of myrrh and aloes, about a hundred pound weight." *John 19:39*

Numbers 24:5-6

Song of Solomon 4:13-15

Research on Sandalwood/Aloes
(Santalum album)

Modern science is now beginning to investigate the antiseptic and immune supporting properties of some of the constituents.

90% sesquiterpenes which deprogram miswritten information in the DNA and crosses over the blood-brain barrier to oxygenate the pineal and pituitary glands

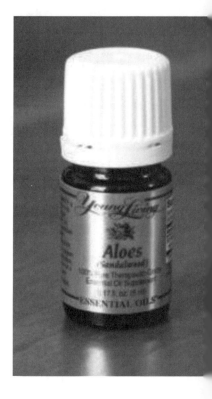

" Taken from "The Healing Oils the Bible" by David Stewart

Ancient Uses of Sandalwood/Aloes

Historically, sandalwood has been recognized for:

- Strengthening the heart and heart fatigue
- Supporting the Lymphatic system
- Calming the nerves
- Skin revitalization
- An aphrodisiac
- Meditation and prayer
- Embalming
- Use in Hemorrhaging

Sandalwood leaves, wood, flowers and sawdust

Modern Uses of Sandalwood/Aloes

- Exquisite skin care
- Enhances deep sleep (stimulates the release of natural melatonin)
- Supportive of female reproductive and endocrine systems
- Apply for urinary tract infections
- Popular cologne for men (extremely attractive to woman)
- May inhibit cervical cancer
- Viral infections (HPV, herpes zoster, herpes simplex)

For sensitive skin mix with Young Livings V-6 in the palm of your hand. Avoid eyes.

Sandalwood Testimonial

"In 2003 my daughter was diagnosed with cervical cancer. She refused conventional medical treatment and I recommend Young Livings therapeutic grade essential oil of Sandalwood. I had read that Sandalwood oil had a 93.1 % kill rate on specific cervical cancer cells without damaging healthy cells. I got her the oil and 18 months later she was cancer free.

What an answer to prayer! "

Christina Campbell O'Fallon, IL

Cassia In Scriptures

- *Psalms 45:8* says "All thy garments smell of myrrh and aloes and cassia. Out of the ivory palaces where by they have made thee glad."
- *Exodus* 30:24 "And of cassia five hundred [shekels], after the shekel of the sanctuary, and of oil olive an hin."
- *Ezekiel 27:19*
- *Job 42:14* ("Kezia" means Cassia.)

Research on Cassia
(cinnamomum cassia)

Cassia showed maximum antibacterial activity against Pseudomonas aeruginosa which is a Gram-negative, aerobic, bacteria. An opportunistic human pathogen.
Indian J Pharm Sci. 2009 Mar;71(2):136-9.

Lee HS. "Inhibitory activity of Cinnamomum cassia bark-derived component against rat lens aldose reductase."

J pharm Sci. 2002 Sep-Dec;5(3):226-30 (Glucose concentrations are often elevated in diabetics and aldose reductase has long been believed to be responsible for diabetic complications involving a number of organs.)

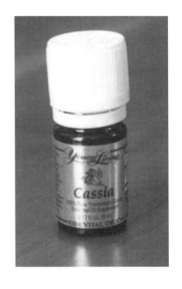

Extracts of Cassia is effective against blood-sucking parasites
PMID: 20306205 [PubMed - as supplied by publisher]

Ancient & Modern Uses of Cassia

- Ingredient in Moses' Holy Anointing Oil
- Diffuse cassia into the air, in the home diffuser to dispel stress and depression
- Immune System Builder
- Anti-inflammatory (COX2 inhibitor)
- Exquisite perfume for both men and woman as it has a tremendous emotional response in the body
- Antibacterial
- Antifungal – fungal infections
- Anticoagulant
- Snakebites
- Common cold
- Kidney troubles

Note: Always use V-6 mixing oil when using Cassia on the skin

Spikenard & Anointing

"Then took Mary a pound of ointment of spikenard, very costly, and anointed the feet of Jesus, and wiped his feet with her hair: and the house was filled with the odour of the ointment."
John 12:3

"There came unto him a woman having an alabaster box of very precious ointment, and poured it on his head, as he sat at meat."
Matthew 26:7

"While the king is at his table my oil of Spikenard send fourth its fragrance."
Song of Solomon 1:12

Song of Solomon 4:13-14, Mark 14:3, Luke 7:37

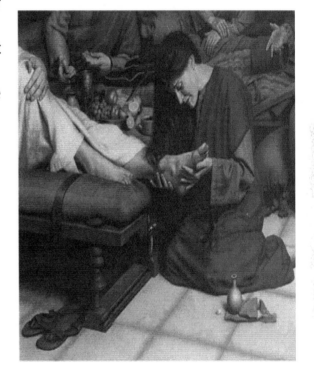

Research on Spikenard
(Nardostachys jatamansi)

- 50% sesquiterpenes
- Has been effective against E. Coli, Listeria (a serious infection caused by eating food contaminated with the bacteria), and salmonella.

Friedman M. Henika PR, Mandrell RE. J. Food Prot. 2002 Oct;65(10):1545-60

- Strengthens the heart and improves circulation

Dietrich Gumbel, PhD.

Ancient & Modern Uses for Spikenard

- Antibacterial
- Antifungal
- Anti-inflammatory
- Nervous tension
- Skin tonic
- Cardiovascular support
- Reduces anxiety
- Migraines
- Perfume
- Relaxant
- Emotionally supporting
- Immune stimulant
- Allergies
- Nausea

Hyssop in Scripture

"And ye shall take a bunch of hyssop and dip it in the blood that is in the basin and strike the lentils and the two side posts with the blood that is in the basin. And none of you shall go out of the door of the house until the morning."
Exodus 12:22

"Purge me with hyssop, and I shall be clean: wash me, and I shall be whiter than snow."
Psalm 51:7

Leviticus 14:4, 6. 49, 51,-52

Numbers 19:6, 18

I Kings 4:33

John 19:29

Hebrews 9:19

Research on Hyssop
(*Hyssopus officinalis*)

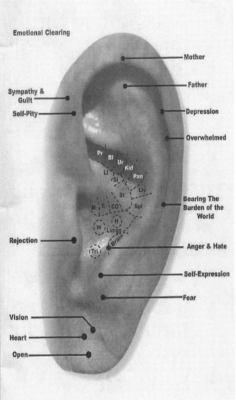

Then shall the priest command to take for him...hyssop: And the priest shall pour of the oil into the palm of his own left hand... put of the oil that is in his hand upon the tip of the right ear of him that is to be cleansed, and upon the thumb of his right hand, and upon the great toe of his right foot..." Leviticus 14:15-28

According to the auricular emotions chart, the top of the right ear is the nerve ending (VitaFlex) point for guilt and the right thumb and right big toe are the nerve ending points for the pineal gland in the center of the brain, where the emotions are stored in the body. By applying this ancient wisdom today, we can experience emotional cleansing and healing with this application of hyssop.

Ancient & Modern Uses for Hyssop

- Ancient and Modern day anti-plague oil
- Respiratory Infections
- Viral infections
- Parasites
- Breaks up mucous
- Anti-inflammatory
- Coughs, colds, asthma and fevers
- Strengthening and toning the nervous system
- Helps release swallowed emotions
- Antiseptic

Note: Avoid use if epileptic or pregnant

Asthma - Frankincense & Hyssop

"I was over using a rescue inhaler. The Dr. told me I could have killed myself because I was using it too frequently. This was in 2007. I started to use Frankincense and Hyssop on myself for respiratory relief. I started rubbing those on my feet first, some relief, then on feet and chest, BINGO I can breathe freely without the aid of my inhaler. I have not had Asthma problems again. What a blessing it is to have God's oils in our presence!"

Loretta Shipp, E. St Louis, IL

How Frankincense and Hyssop saved me from Asthma attacks.

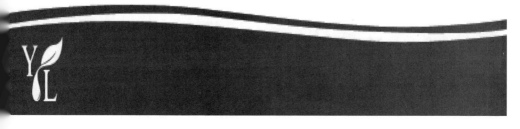

Myrtle In Scripture

"I will plant in the wilderness the cedar, the shittah tree, and the **myrtle**, and the oil tree; I will set in the desert the fir tree, *and* the pine, and the box tree together"
Isaiah 41:19

"Instead of the thorn shall come up the fir tree, and instead of the brier shall come up the **myrtle** tree: and it shall be to the LORD for a name, for an everlasting sign *that* shall not be cut off. "
Isaiah 55:13

- *Zechariah 1:8*
- *Zechariah*
- *Nehemiah 8:15*

Research on Myrtle
(Myrtus communis L.)

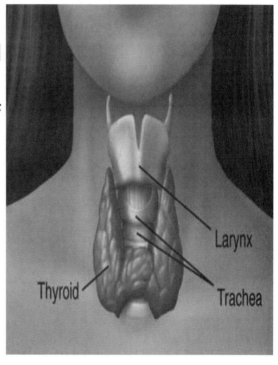

Myrtle has been researched by Dr. Daniel Pénoël for normalizing hormonal imbalances of the thyroid and ovaries, as well as balancing the hypothyroid.

Myrtle has also been researched for its soothing effects on the respiratory system.

Historical Fact of Esther

In the original Hebrew Esther was originally translated Hadassah, meaning myrtle, and received her name of Esther when she entered the royal harem.

Ancient & Modern Uses of Myrtle

- Supports the Thyroid
- Use for throat, lung, and sinus infections
- Prostate problems
- Acne, blemishes, bruises, oily skin, psoriasis
- Muscle spasms
- General hormone balance

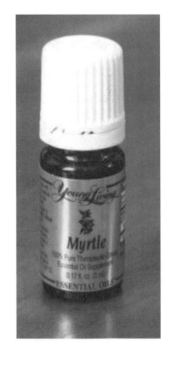

Note: Suitable for children

MUSIC AND MYRTLE

"I am a music minister and an avid student of ancient Hebrew customs. I discovered that in the time of King Solomon's Temple , the singers would anoint their throats with the Oil of Myrtle and the musicians would anoint their instruments with Frankincense. I decided to do this before my own time of worship. I found it was necessary to apply the Myrtle Oil at least 30 minutes before the first song, because the Oil helps to expel the excess mucus in the throat and clear the vocal chords in preparation for singing. The Ancient Oils of the Bible are still as relevant today for singers and musicians as they were 3,000 years ago!"

Reverend Janet McBride, Phoenix , AZ

Rose of Sharon in Scripture

"I am the Rose of Sharon, *and* the lily of the valleys."
Song of Solomon 2:1

"Cistus (Rose of Sharon) has a rich biblical heritage: In ancient times it was collected from the hair of goats that browsed among the bushes. This rose like flower is found in the fertile plains between Jaffa and Mt Carmel in Israel: and because this fertile plain is called Sharon the cistus is also called the Rose of Sharon."

Scriptural Essence
By Janet McBride

Ancient & Modern Uses Rose of Sharon (Cistus)

- Regeneration of cells
- Antiviral
- Antibacterial
- Prevents hemorrhaging
- Reduces inflammation
- Urinary tract infections
- Immune enhancing
- Arthritis
- Calming to the nerves
- Elevates the emotions
- Wounds
- Wrinkles
- Supports healthy sinuses
- Supports sympathetic nervous system

Onycha in Scripture
(Styrax Benzion)

prized for healing since Biblical times. "And the Lord said unto Moses, Take unto thee sweet spices, stacte, and onycha, and galbanum; sweet spices with pure frankincense."

Exodus 30:34

Ancient & Modern Uses of Onycha

Onycha has a wonderful aroma of vanilla because it contains vanilla aldehyde, also found in the vanilla plant.

- Exquisite Perfume
- Antiseptic
- May help control blood sugar levels
- Comforting, soothing and calming when massaged into the skin
- Bronchitis, colds, coughs and sore throats
- Dermatitis and skin wounds
- Colic and Constipation

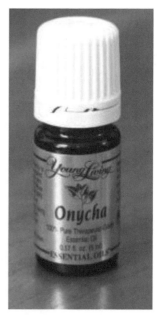

(For sensitive skin mix with Young Livings V-6 in the palm of your hand)

Galbanum in the Scriptures

"The Lord said to Moses: Take sweet spices, stacte,[another name for myrrh] and onycha, and galbanum, sweet spices with pure frankincense and make an incense blended as by the perfumer, seasoned with salt, pure and holy; and you shall beat some of it into powder, and put part of it before the covenant in the tent of meeting where I shall meet with you; it shall be for you most holy. When you make incense according to his composition, you shall not make for yourselves; it shall be regarded by you as holy to the Lord."
Exodus 30:34-36

History of Galbanum
(Ferula gummosa)

The Jewish Talmud states "every communal fast that doesn't include the sinners is not a communal fast."

It is believed that this passage solves the mystery of why this less than fragrant, earthy oils was part of the holy anointing oil

Christ said "I Didn't come for the righteous, I came for the sinners." Galbanum represents those people that need redemption.

When you diffuse this as a single oil into the air of your home, it helps to bring harmony and balance. It's a very harmonic oil.

Ancient & Modern Uses of Galbanum

Abscesses
Acne
Asthma
Chronic coughs
Cramps
Indigestion
Muscular aches and pains
Scar tissue, wrinkles, wounds
Emotional balancing
Menstrual Problems
Galbanum can be used topically and orally as well as diffused.

This is a non-toxic and non-irritating oil to the skin.

Although Galbanum has a low vibrational frequency, when combined with other oils like frankincense or sandalwood, the frequency rises dramatically. It is called a sacrificial fragrance that allows for the shedding of old ideas and attitudes. Its odor helps in seeing the path ahead. It is grounding, yet leads to a surrendering to God.

How to Begin Enjoying Your 12 Oils of Ancient Scripture Collection

Retail $262.83 USD

Wholesale Price $199.75 USD

To receive wholesale pricing first order:

Start Living Enrollment Kit $40.00
Code # 3693

Savings of $63.08

Code #3143

To Order : www.oilsfromheaven.com,
Email: oilsfromheaven@yahoo.com
Phone 1-928-777-9107

V-6 Mixing Oil

V-6 Enhanced Vegetable Oil Complex is used to dilute certain essential oils and is highly recommended to be used with this exquisite collection of Biblical oils. A few drops of V-6 in the palm of your hand with a few drops of the highly concentrated essential oil. Mix and apply.

This beautiful mixing oil is a blend of Coconut Oil, Sesame Seed Oil, Grape Seed Oil, Sweet Almond Oil, Wheat Germ Oil, Sunflower Seed Oil, and Olive Fruit Oil.

Code #3031
Retail: $23.36 USD
Wholesale: $17.75 USD

Resources for Your Education

Experiencing the 12 Oils of Ancient Scripture CD
with Teri Secrest
http://crowndiamondtools.com

How to Teach the 12 Oils of Ancients Scripture DVD
by Teri Secrest
http://crowndiamondtools.com

http://www.ylwisdom.com

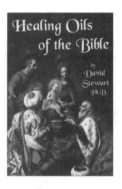

www.abundanthealth4u.com

Spread healing around the World

Teri Secrest in the Philippines teaching the children in an orphanage how to use the ancient oils".

Let's share this ancient knowledge with others, bringing joy and more vibrant and healthy living around the world.

To Order : www.oilsfromheaven.com,
Email: oilsfromheaven@yahoo.com
Phone 1-928-777-9107

Order Dr. Francis Myles's Bestselling Book

"The Order of Melchizedek"

...the book that has received worldwide acclaim!

You have NEVER been to a "Life Changing School of Ministry" like our 3-day weekend encounters!

We encourage you to go to "http://www.theomlu.com" www.theomlu.com and request an invitation to our one of a kind "Leadership University." A Cutting edge school of ministry on Kingdom Living, Kingdom Theonomics, Marketplace Ministry, The Order of Melchizedek and The 7 Mountains of Culture just to name a few. Listen to what our Alumni have to say about their time at one of our 3-day Intensive School of Ministry. Dr. Francis Myles, Chancellor.

Alumni Endorsements

The Order of Melchizedek Conference with Dr. Francis Myles is a must for anyone seeking the deeper things in their faith. I had the blessing of attending this conference with my 21-year-old daughter, Elizabeth. We came away with a wonderful understanding of who we are as daughters of the King. We learned how to implement these principles as we propel forward to our higher callings. We also learned valuable Biblical principles of doing business according to the order of Melchizedek, which is in the highest of integrity. This is a very small investment of time for an enormous return.

> – Teri Secrest, CEO
> *Essential Oils Healthline Inc*
> *"http://www.oilsfromheaven.com/"*
> *www.oilsfromheaven.com*
> *"Changing the way the world thinks about health care"*

The Order of Melchizedek Leadership University is a "Must Attend"! As a twenty-one year old passionately seeking after the heart of God I had a lot of gaps and questions in my mind before attending the University. How can I fully step into my destiny? How much is my life and my work worth to God? Does God need me? How can I be a Christian and work in the marketplace? What's the difference between being a Christian and a Kingdom Citizen? All these questions and more were answered for me. My life now has more order. I wake up in the morning knowing I have a purpose and that through my Lord and Savior I can easily cross over all barriers that used to stand in my path to a life of victory. Understanding the Order of Melchizedek will transform your life forever!

> – Elizabeth Williams
> *Personal Health and Wellness Coach*

http://www.elizabethwilliams.vibrantscents.com/"www.elizabethwilliams.vibrantscents.com
Professional Vocalist and Pianist
http://www.elizabethrosesings.com/www.elizabethrosesings.com
http://www.myspace.com/elizabethrosesings"www.myspace.com/elizabethrosesings

Notes

Notes

Notes

Notes

Notes

Notes

Notes